FRENCH THOUGHT
IN THE
EIGHTEENTH CENTURY

BY
DANIEL MORNET 1878-
PROFESSOR OF FRENCH LITERATURE AT THE SORBONNE

TRANSLATED BY
LAWRENCE M. LEVIN
COLUMBIA UNIVERSITY

NEW YORK
PRENTICE-HALL, INC.
1929

16/95

TRANSLATOR'S PREFACE

Professor Daniel Mornet is highly regarded by Romance scholars throughout the world. He is professor of French Literature at the Sorbonne in Paris; he has written a number of highly esteemed books [1] and articles that are noted for their critical acumen, their breadth of view, and their unusual impartiality; he is the editor of the scholarly *Review of French Literary History*. Above all, he is one of the chief proponents of the so-called historical method of literary criticism. As Professor Mornet explains,[2] this method represents a reaction against the excessive generalizing tendencies of a past generation; it avoids hypotheses so vast that "verification is humanly impossible";

[1] The more important of these works are: *The Attitude Toward Nature in France from J.-J. Rousseau to Bernardin de Saint-Pierre*, Paris, 1907; *The French Alexandrine in the Second Half of the 18th Century*, Toulouse, 1907; *The Natural Sciences in France in the 18th Century*, Paris, 1911; *The Eighteenth Century (from 1750 to 1789)* in the *History of French Literature*, edited by J. Bédier and P. Hazard, Paris, 1924; *Romanticism in France in the 18th Century*, 2nd edition, Paris, 1925; *A General History of French Literature*, Paris, 1925; *A History of the Great Works of French Literature*, Paris, 1925; a critical edition of J.-J. Rousseau's *Modern Héloise*, 4 vols., Paris, 1925-6; *French Thought in the 18th Century*, Paris, 1926; *A History of Contemporary French Literature and Thought*, Paris, 1927.

[2] In the *Romanic Review*, Vol. XIX (1928), pp. 324-327.

it emphasizes the validity of researches on a comparatively modest scale. These researches are to be as nearly authentic as human industry and human ingenuity can make them; and the hypotheses that will be based upon them will rest on a surer foundation than in the past and will not be so easily overthrown at the whim of a subsequent generation.

The "historical method" has been adopted by Professor Mornet in the present work. He presents his facts—and they are unusually abundant and comprehensive—in orderly, precise, and convincing fashion, and with the most admirable impartiality; and the generalizations that follow from the facts become more or less self-evident. Thus the eighteenth century is represented neither as a philosophical crusade "without fear and without reproach" against the monsters of despotism and Catholicism nor as a nightmare of gross indecency, irreverence and ultimate anarchy. Instead, the century is represented with all its greatness and its pettiness, its philosophical insight and its gross exaggeration, its genuine spirituality and its mawkish sentimentalism. Above all, it is not considered as an isolated period in the history of literature and philosophy; it is portrayed as a natural outgrowth and consequence of that splendid but in some respects disastrous "great century" that preceded it and also as a treasure-house of ideas from which the nineteenth century

borrowed freely in the course of its scientific,
literary, and spiritual development.

L. M. L.

CONTENTS

viii CONTENTS

AUTHOR'S FOREWORD

I have not proposed in this brief work to write a more or less comprehensive history of eighteenth century French literature; it already exists in sundry general works. I have written one history of the sort myself [1] and it is not my intention to write another in some 220 pages. On the other hand, no one has as yet composed a methodical and coherent history of French thought in the eighteenth century. Such attempts as have been made hitherto in this field have not been very successful, either because the history of thought has been outlined in connection with the history of art, taste, and individual temperament or else because the study of the great men of the period has caused the author to rather neglect the study of the general tendencies of thought and of public opinion. In other cases, the treatment of the subject has been incomplete and partial. I have therefore attempted to write the history not of a few great men or of a few literary types but of the intellectual and moral life of the nation from about 1700 to 1789.

[1] [Cf. note 1, Translator's Preface. The translator's notes are indicated throughout by brackets.]

I have endeavored to be an impartial historian of the period. I have tried to avoid categorical statements to the effect that this or that condition was good or bad. In each case I have merely indicated (such at least has been my aim) exactly what conditions were; I have then left it for the reader to draw his own conclusions in the matter.

I take it for granted that most of my readers know the salient facts of the literary history of the period and that they have a general idea of its more important works. Of course it would be impossible for me to give a circumstantial account of each author or each literary work without breaking the continuity of the exposition. However, the works of this series [2] are also intended for those who have no knowledge of—or who have forgotten—the subject with which they would become acquainted. Therefore, at the beginning of certain chapters I have given a concise but adequate account of the life and works of the principal authors whose contributions to French thought I have analyzed. A short alphabetical index has been provided to enable the reader to find the requisite information about any given author.

D. M.

[2] [Prof. Mornet's book is one of the volumes of the *Collection Armand Colin*.]

PART I

SURVIVALS OF THE CLASSICAL SPIRIT

CHAPTER I

LITERARY DOCTRINES

Historical note.—Voltaire was the dramatic and epic poet of the eighteenth century. As a matter of fact, up to about 1750 many readers were, or pretended to be, unaware of the fact that he was a philosopher, and devoted themselves only to his poetical "masterpieces."

Voltaire (anagram of Arouet l[e] J[eune]) was born in Paris in 1694. His father left him a small fortune, and he occupied himself with worldly pleasures and literary studies. In 1719 he produced with great success the tragedy of *Œdipus*. Certain impertinent acts of his, and an altercation with the chevalier de Rohan, caused him to be exiled to England (1726-1729). On his return, he produced other tragedies (*Brutus*, 1730; *Zaïre*, 1732) and composed a fine historical work, excellently documented, the *History of Charles XII*. Then he gave an account of his experiences in England and the philosophical teachings that he had imbibed there in the *Philosophical Letters* (1734). The work was banned and Voltaire took refuge at Cirey, at the château of the marquise de Châtelet. He scored further success on the stage with *Alzire* (1736), *Mérope* (1743), and other plays of his. For some years he still attempted to achieve prominence in official circles and court life, and was named gentleman-in-waiting, historiographer of France, and academician. Envious of Crébillon, he produced three tragedies (*Semi-*

3

ramis, Rome Preserved, Catiline) in order to rival him. But his audacity was disquieting to the authorities. He felt himself suspected and therefore accepted the invitation of Frederick II of Prussia, arriving at Potsdam in 1750. (For the second period of the life of Voltaire, cf. p. 52.)

Of the other dramatic authors of the eighteenth century only one deserves mention, not because of his merit but because of the admiration he aroused; I refer to Crébillon (1674-1762), who set the fashion of "tragedies of terror": *Atreus and Thyestis* (1707), *Electra* (1708), *Rhadamistus and Zenobia* (1711), and others.

The principal writers of comedies were: Regnard (1655-1709), whose comedies are still amusing because of their sprightliness and their wit: *The Gambler* (1696), *The Amorous Follies* (1704), *The Sole Heir* (1708); Lesage (1688-1747), who wrote a great number of plays for the Italian Theatre of Paris and a good comedy of manners, *Turcaret* (1709), which is a biting satire on the financiers of the day; Dancourt (1661-1725), who has left us plays that are mediocre in style and plot, but in which there is a quite powerful portrayal of contemporary customs and manners (*The Fashionable Cavalier, The Aristocratic Burghers, The Stockjobbers,* and others). (For the comedies of Marivaux, cf. p. 21.)

The principal novelists were: Lesage, whose *Devil on Two Sticks* (1707) was a rather close imitation of a Spanish novel by Guevara. His *Gil Blas* (1715-1747) is likewise an imitation of several Spanish works; it has a rather fantastic and complicated plot but it contains one vivid character, that of Gil Blas, and sundry picturesque portrayals of customs. The abbé Prévost (1697-1763) led the life of a restless adventurer. His *Memoirs of a Man of Quality* (1728-1731) and his *English Philosopher, or the Memoirs of Cleveland* (1732) are highly adventurous novels of intrigue, in which, however, he depicts tormented souls that are really quite romantic. *Manon Lescaut,* a short and gripping tale, appeared in 1731. (For the novels of Marivaux, cf. p. 22.)

Vauvenargues (1715-1747) was an obscure officer who had visions of military renown. But during the terrible retreat from Prague (1742), he contracted an illness that ruined his health and condemned him to inaction. He died at thirty-two years of age. He published an *Introduction to the Knowledge of the Human Mind,* followed by *Reflections on Sundry Matters* (1746).

The teaching of the colleges.—The spirit of the eighteenth century is evidently quite different from the classical spirit. Neither Voltaire, nor Diderot, nor Rousseau, nor Chénier would have been understood by Boileau, Racine, or La Fontaine. However, not all literary canons and doctrines were simultaneously renewed. Some of them were prolonged without much alteration until the Revolution, and even survived it; they were those particular doctrines that college teachers had developed and taught. And one should not belittle the profound influence that these teachers may exercise when they are convinced that they possess the truth.

Until 1762 it was the Jesuits who directed the majority of colleges; their method of instruction in 1762 was more or less exactly that of 1660. It is true that the colleges of the University, those of the Oratorians, the Doctrinaries, and others, kept more or less abreast with the times after 1740 and 1750. Furthermore, after 1762 a wave of reform swept over the institutions from which the Jesuits had just been ousted; we shall show the importance of these reforms. However, certain traditions, certain convictions, subsisted until the end of the century and even after that time; and it was precisely such traditions and convictions that profoundly influenced, if not the philosophers of the time, at least the poets, the dramatists, and the "devotees of good taste" of the eighteenth century.

To begin with, the goal of teaching is still rhetoric. Whether this teaching be exclusively in Latin, as in the case of the Jesuits, or whether it give due place to French, as in the case of the Oratorians and quite generally after 1762, it culminates in the rules of rhetoric and the discourses or amplifications in which these rules are applied. The essence of this rhetoric is that one does not write to express what one feels or even what one thinks; it is not necessary to have impressions or opinions. The subjects proposed are: "A young man ought to desire death."—"The remorse that overwhelmed Nero after the murder of his mother." When Diderot entered the college of Harcourt, the first subject that he was assigned was: "The discourse with which the serpent tempted Eve." At fourteen years of age or at eighteen, one generally does not think much about early death or the remorse of parricides. But that matters little. Others have thought about these matters, others whose names are Vergil, Tacitus, Bossuet, or Massillon. It suffices at the outset to *remember* what they have said. After which it suffices to utilize these literary recollections in accordance with the principles and rules formulated by the masters of the art of rhetoric—Cicero, Quintilian, Boileau, Father Rapin—and perfected indefatigably by generations of professors who have dictated the contents of their rhetoric notebooks. As a matter of fact, the entire system of education—and, as we have seen, rhetoric represents its culmination—is certainly not calculated to teach the student to think for himself. Instead, he is taught the thoughts of others and the art of giving them not the most original but the "most perfect" application, that is to say, the one most in conformity with the rules. To write or to think is to imitate: to imitate, with respect to subject matter, the masters of literature from Vergil to Racine and Mascaron; to imitate, with respect to form, the precepts of the professors of art, from Cicero to Boileau, Father Buffier, or the abbé Batteux.

Education will undergo a definite transformation toward 1770 or 1780; but this transformation will not be as thoroughgoing as it might appear to be. The old rhetoric will be discussed, condemned, often reviled. But generally it will continue to influence even the philosophers and their disciples. After 1762 there will be an official condemnation of the tragedies, comedies, and "frivolous" ballets that the Jesuits had their students give every year. In their place there will be inaugurated public exercises resembling the "programs" of the present time. But whether these exercises be given under the auspices of the University or the Oratorians or independent teachers, all or almost all of them might well have been approved by the Jesuits of the year 1660. The young orators of the college of Bayeux debate the following problem: "Which is the most wretched: a sculptor who loses his hands, an orator deprived of his tongue, a painter who becomes blind, or a young man who is deaf?" They argue in Latin. The college of Bourges is more modern. Three students, Sacrot, Masson, and Delalande argue in French; and the subject bears on a modern topic. It deals with the war of the Russians against the Ottomans. The two friends, Alexiovitch and Basilovitch, have been made prisoners. Alexiovitch is released so that he may console his mother who has become blind because of weeping. He has sworn to return; Basilovitch has offered his own life as security for the fulfillment of his friend's oath. The mother desires to keep her son with her. Of the students named above, Sacrot speaks for the mother, Delalande for Alexiovitch, Masson for Basilovitch. But the Boyards who are being discussed are no more Russian than the Bajazet of Racine is Turkish. It is all a mere adaptation of the tale of Damon and Pythias: it is the traditional rhetoric.

The major poetic types.—It will never be known whether this type of pedagogy prolonged the existence of the prevalent literary canons and doctrines or whether it was literature that prolonged the influence of pedagogy. But at any rate, pedagogy and literature give each other mutual support, and their combined force of resistance, in spite of philosophy and "revolutions" in literary taste, be-

comes invincible. Until the Revolution and
even after it, the major poetic types—tragedy,
comedy, epic poetry, descriptive poetry, odes
—will be written according to the rules taught
by the colleges. A tragedy of the college of
Romorantin or an ode of Father Labat and
the tragedies of Voltaire or the odes of Lebrun-Pindare differ only in their greater or
lesser mediocrity.

Voltaire, indeed, introduced or tried to introduce many novelties in his tragedies. He remembered that he was a philosopher and that
it behooved him, in writing *Zaïre* or *Moham-
med* or *Alzire* or the *Parsees*, to combat fanaticism and to defend "humanity." Likewise
he perceived that his contemporaries were
discovering that they were really quite sentimentally inclined; therefore instead of en-
deavoring to inspire them equally with "terror"
and "pity," he sought to write "touching"
plays. He also perceived that the spectators were becoming wearied and that they
must be given a little of that novelty that they
were beginning to find in Shakespeare, Lillo,
and Moore. Consequently he essayed, if not
every device, at least all sorts of devices: historical tragedy with tableaux and without any
love-plot (*The Death of Cæsar*), national

tragedy (*Tancred, Adelaide du Guesclin*), exotic tragedy (*Alzire, The Orphan of China*). He wished to "appeal to the eye" and even to "harass the nerves" of the spectators with stage sets and mechanical apparatus: the escutcheons and oriflammes of a tournament, chains, a ghost, turbans, and scimitars. He desired to write tragedies that were to be "new" and even "modern."

But he wrote nothing but mediocre and uninspired college exercises. Inevitably, and perhaps because he was utterly lacking in dramatic genius, he composed *Zaïre* or *Tancred* or the *Parsees* just as he had composed while at college the "Remorse of Nero" or the "Discourse of the Serpent." Inevitably he remembered both Corneille and Racine, even Thomas Corneille and La Motte-Houdart. The most eloquent or even the most natural passages of his dramatic compositions are mere centos or imitations. Even the plots of his plays are really influenced by all those who have reasoned about the unities, about tragic love, about the sublime. He contrives his plots with studious and meticulous application; he listens to, in fact provokes, counsel of every sort; he adapts and retouches incessantly. But he never corrects for the purpose of being himself or of creating truth. And his apparently bold innovations are but copies of Corneille, of Shakespeare, of Crébillon, of many others. His style is equally labored and timorous. It is "refined" and " exalted"; that is to say, we have the words, the images, and the figures of a Racine, revised and corrected by a pedantic and meticulous master of good taste.

Even Voltaire, who is talented, shrewd, and industrious, fails; as for the others, they composed only platitudes or sheer nonsense. All or almost all tried their hand at composing dramas or, more specifically, tragedies. For tragedy is the preëminently "noble" literary type; it is tragedy that bestows the widest renown. Crébillon the Elder, who had no knowledge of character, who was completely lacking in good taste and even in judgment, was celebrated because he had utilized the dramatic element of "terror" with more audacity than Corneille, because he heaped up frenzies, murders, and imprecations in his "sinister" tragedies. An adroit opportunist like Marmontel, a studious worker like Lemierre, a timid, melancholy creature like Colardeau, a respectable sort of man like de Belloy—all reap their share of applause. But the terror of

Hypermnestre, the pathos of *Caliste*, the patriotism of the *Siege of Calais* are alike utterly unoriginal; it is always merely a matter of imitating, or at most of adapting, Corneille, Racine, or Voltaire, with certain "bold" innovations that are merely timid and awkward borrowings from Shakespeare and from the drama. The best tragedies are the works of mere rhetoricians.

One may say as much for comedy. To be sure, it often arouses the interest of the historian. Dancourt and Lesage have left us some picturesque and quite vigorously limned portrayals of a society in which vices, adroitly manipulated, are beginning to bestow profits and honors. The *Turcaret* of Lesage is not a masterpiece by any means; still the figure of the unscrupulous financier, so utterly duped by love, remains a type and not merely a literary document. But the comedy of manners itself gradually disappears. It obliges one to observe for oneself; and it is considered much safer and, above all, more worthy of the Muses to imitate the characterization and the style of a Terence or a Molière. The comedy of manners degenerates into the ultra-popular comedy of Vadé. The comedy of character attempts to depict the *Gambler* (Regnard), the

Mischief Maker (Gresset), the *Versifier*
(*Metromania*, by Piron), the *Boaster* (Des-
touches), the *Scold*, and the *Gossip*, and so on.
But we have mere silhouettes which have a
striking family resemblance. From the valets
and the maidservants, who are precisely those
of Molière, to the "rogue" or the "gambler,"
we have only gossipy creatures whose function
it is to serve as illustrations of sundry moral-
istic definitions. When college professors write
comedies about the *Rake* or the *Listless One*,
they put into their efforts about as much vitality and accuracy as one finds in the comedies
of Piron or Gresset.

The chief poetic type, the epic, has likewise
fallen upon evil days. To be sure, the eighteenth century believed in all good faith that
it had produced an epic masterpiece, the *Henriade* of Voltaire. Innumerable editions disseminate its glory. It is read, cited, commented
upon in the colleges; it is given as an academic
prize almost as frequently as the treatises of
the abbé Batteux or the *Lent* of Massillon. It
is genuinely believed that the *Henriade* ap-
proaches Homer and that it equals Vergil.
And indeed it is quite the equivalent of Vergil; it belongs in the same category. If one
disregards what is not to be found in the singer

of Mantua, that is, the eulogy of the humane and tolerant Henry IV, the *Henriade*, like the *Æneid*, is composed almost entirely of reminiscences and it observes the rules most exactly. And when it is no longer Vergil, it is Lucan or Tasso or Ariosto. It is everybody but Voltaire.

The triumph of Voltaire almost discouraged imitators; perhaps one felt a vague misgiving at the thought of imitating the masterpiece of imitation. And in order to secure a new field for creation, the "descriptive poem" was invented toward 1760. Saint-Lambert wrote *The Seasons* (1769), Lemierre *Painting* (1769), Roucher *The Months* (1779), Delille *The Gardens* (1782), and Chénier began his *Hermes*, or *America*. They pretended, of course, to introduce "new thoughts": the eulogy of agriculture and nature, the discoveries of the sciences, humanity and benevolence, justice and tolerance. But the oldest poetical formulas of the colleges were still employed.

Lyric poetry is even more degraded, if that were possible. At the beginning of the century Jean-Baptiste Rousseau is considered an out-and-out genius. As a matter of fact, his art consists of adroitly applying the principles of the poetic theory of the sublime. He is cited in the colleges for the same reason that the *Henriade* is cited, because he is as excellent a student of the classics as Voltaire. And it is because Lebrun is a proficient student of the classics that his contemporaries, without meaning to be ironical, call him Lebrun-Pindare. Lebrun, indeed, has introduced into his life that fantastic disorder that toward 1780 is beginning to be considered as an indication of genius. But nothing of this fine spirit of independence penetrates his odes and poems. The very best of them are motivated and copied according to all the rules of academic tradition.

Thus, in spite of the *Encyclopedia*, philosophy, and "revolutions" in thought, the classical spirit, or at least a certain classical spirit, subsists throughout the century. It is this spirit that aims to make of literature and good taste a science with certain definite principles or formulas, which one has merely to utilize skillfully. The colleges teach this science; writers and professors perfect it. The poets have no other duty than that of applying it. Unfortunately, their highest meed of praise is: "studious application."

In spite of a political revolution and a religious revolution, or rather, renovation, a last revolution, Romanticism, will be required to definitely overthrow classical tradition.

The analytical novel.—There was, fortunately, a literary type which Aristotle, Cicero, and Quintilian had not discussed, of which neither Vergil, nor Horace, nor any great ancient writer had left any specimen, which college teachers did not mention because they considered it frivolous or corrupting: that was the novel. The novel was not one of the major literary types; it was, above all, a source of entertainment. And it was precisely that feature that saved it from rhetoric and from rules. It was able to profit by the classical spirit without perishing under its tyranny. Classical literature had attempted to penetrate the secret impulses of the passions; it had devoted itself to psychology. To as great an extent as Racine or Molière or La Rochefoucauld, Mme de la Fayette had studied the conflict of love and duty, of passion and self-esteem. And neither Boileau, nor Rapin, nor Rollin, nor Batteux had thought of establishing the rules of this type of analysis when it was made in prose and not in verse, in a novel and not in a tragedy. Thus Lesage, Marivaux, the abbé Prévost, and, at the end of the century, Laclos, were able to write original novels, any one of which is superior to all the epic, lyric, and tragic poems of the century.

Of course, their work is not entirely classical in spirit. In the *Gil Blas* of Lesage there is very often a disdain for good taste and the proprieties, a tendency to caricature, and a popular gusto, that suggest the tavern rather than the *salons* or the Academy. In writing a novel Lesage puts himself at his ease, much as he would do at a drinking bout. The plots of his novels take decided liberties; the adventures of Gil Blas are sometimes improbable. Those of the greater part of the abbé Prévost's heroes, with the exception of the characters of Manon Lescaut, are even more so; for they take Cleveland, the dean of Killerine, and others through many an "awe-inspiring tempest" to the dread abodes of savages and to desolate isles. Besides, these heroes of Prévost have not genuinely classical souls. They have "invincible" and causeless fits of melancholy and a certain zest for suffering, without any possible source of relief, that make them the spiritual ancestors of the Obermanns and the Renés of the following century. To be sure, there is nothing of these singular adventures or of this romanticism in Marivaux, but one does find in him a certain popular taste and certain curious details that would have pleased neither the *salons* of the great century nor

Boileau. His Marianne lives with a seamstress and the seamstress quarrels with a coachman. His upstart peasant is a genuine peasant who penetrates into a very humble class of society, depicted in its devastating mediocrity.

And yet, in spite of realism, in spite of the complication of plot and the "gloomy atmosphere," *Gil Blas, Manon Lescaut, The Life of Marianne, The Upstart Peasant* are classical works and their merit, which is great, is particularly a classical merit. Their heroes are represented accurately, not so much in their costumes, their gestures, and their physical peculiarities as in their moral traits and idiosyncrasies. They make a conscious effort to know themselves well and to explain themselves clearly. And they succeed because in the midst of perils or in the most embarrassing situations they are still capable of lucidity of thought. Gil Blas is not a very heroic personage; he often passively submits to fate. But he succeeds because of his lucky star, and chiefly because he always knows what he is and whither he is bound. Marianne is so eager to know herself well that she seems to be constantly inventing minutiæ of self-analysis for the pleasure of discerning their nuances. The upstart peasant is successful because he knows very exactly how to use his knowledge of himself and of the others.

Through the medium of the novel one of the forms of the classical spirit, psychological analysis, will persist throughout the eighteenth century and will culminate in the *Dangerous Acquaintances* of Choderlos de Laclos and in the novels of Stendhal.

One finds this same taste for analysis in the works of Vauvenargues. Not everything therein is classical; and his maxims are far removed from those of La Rochefoucauld. Vauvenargues is a "Stoic" and not a Christian; he is passionate and neither a skeptic nor a Cartesian. For him the highest aim in life does not lie in the pious virtues, nor is the highest achievement of intelligence the possession of lucid ideas. A great soul, for him, is self-sufficient without God; and great souls are passionate souls. One might even conceive of a moral code in which each might follow his inclination without restraint, and wisely withal. Yet the entire aim of his life is to understand himself, and his ideal is a lucid will-to-action. He dominates his sensibility; he does not abandon himself to it. If his ideas are no longer classical, his method is still classical.

CHAPTER II

THE SOCIETY SPIRIT

Historical note.—The principal *salons* of the first half of the century are those of the duchesse de Maine (1700-1718), frequented by the free-thinkers; of the marquise de Lambert; of Mme de Tencin, a great lady whose life was very adventurous at first and who succeeded Mme de Lambert; of Mme du Deffand (after 1730), who was hardly fond of philosophical discussion— though she was quite skeptical—but who entertained a numerous group of philosophers, including d'Alembert and Turgot. In the second half of the century the most widely known *salons* were those of Mme Geoffrin; of Mlle de Lespinasse, the former reader of Mme du Deffand and a very charming young lady whom Mme du Deffand jealously dismissed; of Mme Helvétius; of Mme d'Holbach; of Mme d'Épinay, the friend of Diderot, Grimm, and Rousseau; finally, the *salon* of Mme Necker.

Marivaux (1688-1763) passed his life frequenting *salons* (particularly those of Mme de Tencin and Mme Geoffrin) and writing. He produced numerous plays, generally with great success, at the *Italian Comic Theatre* or the *French Comic Theatre* (*The Surprise of Love,* 1727; *The Vagaries of Love and Chance,* 1730; *The School for Mothers,* 1732; *The Legacy,* 1736; *The False Confidences,* 1737, etc.). He composed various critical and moral essays published in periodicals (*The French Specta-tor,* 1722-1723, etc.). His novels are: *The Life of Marianne* (1731-1741), unfinished; *The Upstart Peasant* (1735), unfinished.

In the *salons* of the end of the century one finds such writers as Chamfort (1741-1794) and Rivarol (1753-1801), whose reputation is due chiefly to the brilliant and caustic nature of their conversation and to their many short essays, maxims, and thoughts.

Society life.—Society life played as impor-tant a rôle in the eighteenth century as in the seventeenth. At the outset, at least until 1762, the educational system in its entirety prepared one for it. As rhetoric could be applied prac-tically only by lawyers, it was supplemented by the art of living elegantly. "What must I teach my son?" asks the marquis de la Jean-notière, who has but recently acquired his wealth. "To be amiable," replies the friend who is being consulted, "and if he knows the art of pleasing, his knowledge will be com-plete." Of course, Voltaire is jesting. But there are people who take this viewpoint of his quite seriously. "It seems that all the edu-cation that one gives young people," says a treatise of 1751, "is based exclusively upon the art of politeness." Moreover, there is a tend-ency, as in the seventeenth century, to dis-cuss politeness in treatises and dissertations.

In spite of his disdain for M. de la Jean-
notière, Voltaire considers that "this politeness
is not an arbitrary assumption. . . . It is a law
of nature that the French, fortunately, have
cultivated more than other peoples." Lemaître de Claville in an *Essay on the Real
Merit of Man*, a very popular work, places
the polite man immediately after the "noble
soul" and the "lofty spirit." They are in agreement with many others, with Jesuits like
Father Brumoy, with the skeptical d'Argens,
the philosopher, Toussaint, the grave Duclos.
Such works appear as *The Amiable Man* (by
Marin, 1751) and *An Essay on the Necessity
and the Means of Pleasing* (by Moncrif,
1738).

All our great writers attempt to please their
readers, and most of them make a heroic effort to do so. They have had their period of
society life and often it has been quite prolonged. The youth of Voltaire was unreserved-
ly mundane; and his château of Ferney often
becomes a *salon*. Marivaux appears regularly
at the *salons* of Mme de Lambert, Mme de
Tencin, Mme du Deffand, Mme Geoffrin.
Montesquieu, it is true, soon becomes the solitary squire of la Brède. But he begins by being
one of the ornaments of the "dispensaries of

wit" with La Motte and Fontenelle. Rousseau assiduously frequents the *salons* for fifteen years before he definitely "reforms" and flees to the Hermitage. Diderot lays no great store by politeness and he enjoys "solitary meditation"; but he seems nevertheless to be quite fond of the *salons* of Mme du Pusiex, Mme d'Epinay, Mme d'Houdetot, Mme Helvétius, the baron d'Holbach, Mme Necker. Duclos and d'Alembert are really society men. Buffon does not always live at Montbard nor Turgot in his ministry. One meets them at the *salons* of Fanny de Beauharnais, Mme Necker, Mme du Deffand, Mlle de Lespinasse, and others.

The consequences. 1. Gallantry.—This inclination for, or even necessity for, society life entails important consequences. No matter how philosophical the *salons* may be, they are after all *salons*: that is to say, they bring together men and women (young ladies appear but rarely and only toward the end of the century) who are wealthy and unoccupied and who come, not to think, but to seek diversion. This diversion consists primarily of sprightly conversation. But conversation is not diverting in itself unless its themes be pleasurable. And polite society loves one thing above all the rest: that is, to love or at least to speak of love. The frequenters of the *salons* will discuss, therefore, not passion, which is rebellious, austere and calculated to upset the nicely established order of society; not gross sensuality and brutal pleasure, after the fashion of a Rabelais or a Beroald de Verville; but "gallantry." Gallantry is composed of two very different elements which, on the surface, appear to be identical. It is first of all sentimental curiosity, the pleasure of discovering the "hidden sources" and the "secret impulses" of sentiment; it is the search for the ultimate in matters sentimental. It is the pleasure in curiosity that one may grant to oneself even if one be a respectable lady. It is the type of pleasure that Mme Tencin, who did not particularly boast of being virtuous, was wont to offer to her guests: "One lover does not perceive his mistress even if she be present; another sees his mistress even if she be absent: which displays the greater passion?" But gallantry is also, at least in this eighteenth century, sensual pleasure without any real restraint, but with an apparent reserve, that of language. One must speak of base things with elegance, and of gross amusements with distinction. One must give vice the distinction of good company. Almost all our great writers have tried their hand at one or the other of these two types of gallantry or at both.

Marivaux gave its most original type of expression to the former. There is, indeed, something else in his comedies besides *marivaudage*. There is occasionally philosophy: the *Isle of Reason* and the *Isle of the Slaves* discuss the equality of social conditions and the social conventions with a frankness that anticipates Voltaire and occasionally Rousseau. In his more serious comedies, those which have no suggestion of the farcical or of the unreal, in *Prejudice Conquered* or the *False Confidences*, it is the prejudice of social conditions that Marivaux discusses; and he likes to marry off a young lady of the nobility to a commoner. It is not certain, however, that Marivaux took this philosophy very seriously. His chief delight is in love, and gallant love. We should understand by "love" a sentiment that derives its essence not from its violence and its delightful blindness, but from its delicacy and its lucidity. It is decorous love which does not invade human souls to produce exaltation or despair, but which gently takes its place in one's heart after amiably thrusting aside whatever has previously filled it. The lovers analyze and discuss this intrusion; they hesitate between the old order and the new. To yield a place for love, for example, one must relegate one's self-pride to a subordinate position; one must renounce the pride of one's rank, one's reputation as a "dandy," one's pride in being proof against love.

All this is *marivaudage*, which was not entirely the invention of Marivaux, but which had been adopted to a certain extent by the *Précieuses* and which had already appeared in the conversations of the *salons*. But Marivaux endowed it with more subtlety and more accuracy. And to express it he employed a style which is his very own, in which the artificial and the natural, wit and candor, are blended with charming skill. *Marivaudage* was widely discussed and sometimes condemned by eighteenth century writers, perhaps for sheer spite at not being able to imitate it. Many writers, incapable of this supreme species of elegant frivolity, sought to please by delicate analysis of sentiment. The *Temple of Cnidus* of Montesquieu is a "gallant" work, as are certain tales of Voltaire (*The Princess of Babylon*, for example). There is gallantry even in the *Modern Héloïse*, in the relations between Saint-Preux and his cousin, Claire, and sometimes even in the *Natural History* of Buffon. But one finds particularly, even in our greatest writers, the other type of gallantry which consists of decorously considering embarrassing or even obscene topics. It is this type of gallantry which spoils the *Persian Letters*, the *Spirit of the Laws* sometimes, the *Elegies* of Chénier often, and which, if it does not spoil the tales and novels of Voltaire, his pamphlets and his *Philosophical Dictionary*, certainly adds nothing to their merit.

2. Wit.—The only justifications for these improprieties, if one considers that they should have some justification, is the exercise of wit. This wit also owes its origin, in part at least, to society life. It is not the popular wit of a Rabelais nor the sarcasm and morose humor of a Swift, who will not be so much imitated as corrected or adapted. It is the interplay of thought and style: a deliberate attempt not to say things merely in order that they be understood but rather to express them in such a manner that they may cause the greatest amount of æsthetic pleasure. There is wit, or at least an attempt at wit, in most of the works of the eighteenth century, even in the most serious. "In Germany or in England," says Voltaire, "a physicist is a physicist; in France he also would be known as a pleasing writer." "Intimacy with society," says the moralist, J. F. Bernard, "is absolutely essential for the scholar; otherwise he will be considered a pedant." The philosopher has the same obligations as the scholar: "What one calls the philosophy of well-bred people—and everybody would be known as well-bred—is nothing but the secret of combining wisdom and gaiety . . . much reason and a little wit." Often one even preferred much wit to little. The *Discourses Concerning the Plurality of Worlds* by Fontenelle bring astronomy within the mental grasp of a marquise and attempt to disguise science under the mask of badinage. There is much wit, and of the best sort, in the *Philosophical Letters* of Voltaire and yet the abbé Prévost thought that there was not enough. Mme du Deffand reproached the *Spirit of the Laws* for being often merely witty, and she is not entirely wrong. The *Natural History* of Buffon is not always natural—a remark that has already been made in the eighteenth century—and it employs epigram in speaking of the mole and the swan.

Most of the great works of the century, with the exception of those of Voltaire, have not benefited particularly by this display of wit. There is rather too much of the frivolous spirit of a century in which an abbé Pellegrini could publish without occasioning any surprise the *Imitation of Jesus Christ, Arranged in Songs to Operatic and Vaudeville Airs* (1727). But wit did enhance the value of the minor literary types, those innumerable tales, set pieces, compliments, trifles. It is true that the triumph of the minor literary types had certain unpleasant consequences. There is often a tendency to turn away from serious people like Corneille and Racine, in spite of the philosophical spirit or the "sentimental enthusiasm" of the century. Even Molière is slighted: productions of his plays drop from 132 to 66 a year; and the *Doctor in Spite of Himself* and *Monsieur de Pourceaugnac* are preferred to the *Misanthrope* and *Tartuffe*. Tragedy and even comedy are replaced by comic opera, ballets, the theatres of the boulevards, puppet shows, the *Mill of Javelle*, the *Vintage of Suresnes*, the playlets of Audinot and of Nicolet. Entertainers reap a fortune in the service of the great: men like Collé or Carmontelle, who are paid to get up village festivals, "tableaux," or dramatized "proverbs."

But at least the minor literary types often gain an inimitable grace through their devotion to wit. It is thus that Voltaire makes the pamphlet a species of masterpiece as well as a redoubtable weapon. It is not particularly difficult nor clever nor judicious to deride Carmelites, Capuchins, and the Bible. But one improves immeasurably upon mediocre and erroneous ideas when in expressing them one composes the *Instructions of the Superior of the Capuchins of Prague to Father Pediculosus on his Departure for the Holy Land* or the *Canonization of Saint Cucufin, Brother of Ascoli, by Pope Clement XIII and His Appearance in a Vision to Messer Aveline, Citizen of Troyes, Revealed by Messer Aveline Himself.* It is the element of wit that assures the success of the "tales" of the eighteenth century—fairy tales, gallant tales, Greek tales, allegorical tales, moral tales, philosophical tales—the most prosperous literary type of the century. (More than five hundred were published.) It is the element of wit that accounts for the invincible prestige of Voltaire. He has nothing particularly original to say in *Zadig*, or *Micromégas*, or *Candide*, or even in the *Ingenuous Man*. He borrows abundantly from Swift and

from many others. The problems that he considers have been discussed for centuries or are
being discussed by many contemporary
writers. The solutions that he offers are generally neither very profound nor very original.
But it is his wit that endows his work with
such incomparable sprightliness and vitality
and that gives him that "inimitable grace,"
that "something or other" that has been so universally admired for a hundred years and
more.

There is not much vitality in the innumerable *facetiæ* and trifles with which so many poets seek to please their public. But at least,
such a gracious atmosphere pervades these
trifles that they give one the very illusion of
life. "One must be dainty in this century,"
said Colardeau, who was inclined to be melancholy. And all the poetasters from Dorat to
Boufflers, from Voisenon to Parny, vie in seeking the most delicate touches, the slightest nuances. It is the century of "little masterpieces"
which are in truth insignificant; but their in-
significance is veiled by a certain grace, as we
see in the following *Verses of Mme * * *
to Her Daughter, Who Had Sent Her a Cameo
Representing a Cupid Intent upon Catching
a Butterfly in Order to Cut Off Its Wings:*

Le papillon perdant le charme dont il brille
De léger devient lourd, de joli devient laid;
  Il ne reste qu'une chenille.
Quand l'amour, par hasard, fixe certains amants,
  On rit de la métamorphose.
Va, ma fille, crois-moi, des papillons constants
  Fatigueraient bientôt les roses.[1]

Or again, we have this little "philosophical" dialogue of Chamfort: "Are you going to be married?"—"No."—"Why not?"—"Because I should be unhappy."—"Why?"—"Because I should be jealous."—"And why would you be jealous?"—"Because I should be deceived."—'Who told you that you would be deceived?"—"I should be deceived because I should deserve to be deceived."—"And why would you deserve to be deceived?"—"Because I should be married."

Propriety.—Mundane literature, gallant and witty, must, above all, respect propriety. Propriety does not include morality or even common decency: for one may write tales and even compliments that good company finds appropriate and even delightful and yet which are highly inappropriate and even grossly in-

[1] ["The butterfly, once it loses its dazzling charm, is no longer light but clumsy, no longer exquisite but hideous; a mere caterpillar indeed. When Eros, blindly shooting, transfixes certain lovers, one laughs at the fateful change. In very faith, my daughter, butterflies too constant in their devotion would soon weary the roses."]

decent. Propriety is merely the respect for a certain number of subtle and changing rules which in each generation comprise "good tone" and social "standards." It represents the habit of daring nothing, of fearing eccentricity and originality more than vice or crime. To know "good taste" is merely to know the "good taste" of one's fellows. Thenceforth genius lies no longer in power and creative force but in finesse and delicacy. Whatever surprises is displeasing, whatever innovates is shocking. Even when it is desired to stir one's readers and to wield the "thunderbolts of genius," one does so with appropriate restraint and circumspection. "It is necessary," said Crébillon the Elder, "to lead to pity through terror by portraying impulses and emotions that offend neither delicacy nor propriety." Propriety sets its seal upon all things: the murder of Thyestis, the death of Cæsar, or the translations from the Bible. "Her eyes," says the Song of Songs, "are like unto pigeons on the banks of waters laved in milk." Voltaire finds that the appropriate and mundane translation is "Pure ardor gleams in her eyes."

The desire for propriety chastened the mania for foreign things that from the very beginning of the century and in increasing meas-

ure was turning the French toward the literatures of the Orient, England, Scandinavia,
Germany. We shall consider later this im-
petuous curiosity, and we shall indicate the
transformations that it brought about. As a
matter of fact, all this "foreign mania" neither
created nor overthrew anything. All the foreign writers who are read, praised, and imitated are discussed and corrected, very often,
indeed, mutilated. The French spirit borrows
from them only what is already its intellectual
property, and enjoys only what flatters its former tastes. In France, as Voltaire observes
(and his opinion is echoed by many foreigners
who have traveled in France), one must resemble the others, that is, those who belong to
one's own social sphere. In England one does
not concern oneself about the others and one
takes pride in resembling only oneself. Eighteenth century Frenchmen are amazed at this
English individuality; at times, indeed, they
praise it, but they hardly ever imitate it. And
whenever they translate from the English—or
from the Orientals or from the Scandinavians
—they leave untranslated the specifically foreign element that makes a Swift resemble only
a Swift and an Ossian only an Ossian. In the
case of the *Gulliver* of Swift, the dramas of

Shakespeare, the novels of Fielding or Richardson, the poems of Ossian, the *Werther* of Goethe, translations are always mere adaptations. Indeed, on certain occasions there are protests against unfaithful translators. There is a demand for "Shakespeare in his entirety" or "Richardson in his entirety." But even those who take pride in being faithful translators only attenuate falsehood. In his translations Letourneur mutilates rather less than Ducis; he generally avoids mere caricature. But neither his Shakespeare nor his Ossian have much in common with the genuine Shakespeare or Ossian. Propriety is more powerful than romantic taste and Anglomania.

The reaction.—The society spirit and propriety remain powerful until the end of the eighteenth century. But it is certain that after 1760 their dominion is menaced. The reaction against the rules, against "petty spirits," and "false standards of taste" rapidly becomes a violent one. Muralt of Berne "dared to be vulgar when speaking of French politeness." Englishmen like Sherlock, Rutledge, or Moore say the same thing more politely. Rousseau amplifies the accusations of Muralt: it is because Parisian society is worldly and polite that he will flee from it and shut himself up in the Hermitage. To be sure, his indignation is less original than he suspects; Montesquieu and d'Argens had already railed at "false politeness" and the mania for mere wit. Duclos, whose literary success was due to his ability to entertain the frequenters of the *salons*, demonstrates "the unfortunate influence of society upon men of letters." The abbé Coyer, Fougeret de Montbron, and many others compose innumerable allegories, satires, and epigrams which scoff at politeness, propriety, society in general. Paris is called the "Frivolous Isle"; society folk are the "Frivolites." The life of the *salons* and even of the nation itself is a "beautiful dream." But an awakening is solemnly presaged—and feared.

PART II

THE PROLONGATION
AND THE TRANSFORMATION
OF CLASSICAL RATIONALISM

CHAPTER I

THE ORIGINS

Historical note.—Saint-Evremond (1613-1703) was forced into exile after the publication of a disrespectful *Letter on the Treaty of the Pyrenees* (1661). Thereafter he lived in England and in Holland without ceasing to correspond with his friends in France. He sent letters and essays (including *Reflections on the Diverse Character- istics of the Roman People,* which anticipate Montes- quieu), which were supplemented after his death by certain audacious unpublished works (*The Conversation of the Maréchal d'Hocquincourt with Father Canaye*).

Bayle (1647-1706), a Protestant, then a Catholic, then a Protestant again, taught philosophy at Sedan, then at Rotterdam, until he lost his post as a consequence of vio- lent polemics. He published a learned journal called *News of the Republic of Letters* (1684-1687), *Thoughts on the Comet* (1682-1704), etc., and his *Historical and Critical Dictionary* (1697).

Fontenelle (1657-1757) displayed prodigious intellec- tual activity. He attracted attention at the outset by the witty skepticism of his *Dialogues of the Dead* (1683), then by his *Discourses Concerning the Plurality of Worlds,* in which he popularized the Copernican system. His *History of Oracles* was published in 1687. A member of the Academy of Sciences, he wrote elegant and scholarly eulogies of the Academicians, eulogies which caused their

41

studies to become generally known. He was the leading light of many *salons,* including those of Mme de Lambert and Mme Geoffrin.

Almost all the ideas that are dear to the "philosophers" of the eighteenth century had been outlined or suggested as early as the beginning of the seventeenth by those who were not yet known as philosophers but as "free-thinkers."

In truth a goodly number of these free-thinkers set less store by "thinking well" than by "living well." They approved of neither the dogmas nor the moral rules of Christianity nor of Christian philosophy because these rules were severe and because besides curbing their reason they also curbed their pleasures. Cyrano de Bergerac, Dehénault, François Payot de Lignières, Chaulieu, La Fare, in defending their liberty of thought were also defending their right to drink well, to love after their fashion, and to enjoy life to the utmost. In the *salons* of Ninon de Lenclos or of the Temple, at Paris, in that of Mme de Mazarin, at London, the "supreme wisdom" is that which eschews care and seeks sensual pleasure. When old age comes upon such as these, when sensual pleasure vanishes, and illness makes them think of death, most of them follow the example of La Fontaine, Mme de la Sablière, Mme de Villedieu, Mme Deshoulières; they are converted and seek to atone for their libertine past by their ultimate orthodoxy.

Yet there is in this "free thought" a great deal besides gross license and the heedlessness of depraved society people. Gabriel Naudé, Bernier, Mme Deshoulières, Gassendi, Saint-Evremond are very respectable people. Their "freedom" is merely a doctrine. Men like Cyrano, Chapelle, La Fare, and the others are likewise defending a doctrine; if they form a group, if Bossuet and so many others fear them, if they exercise great influence, it is because they have ideas. What are these ideas? First, that it is *unreasonable* to be an Arnault or a Pascal or a Bourdaloue or a Bossuet. Man was not created for the purpose of wearing a hair shirt and administering self-punishment. One does not even gain social order and religious certainty thereby, for those who are stronger rob, terrorize, and exile the weaker, that is to say, Protestants in France or Catholics in Geneva. This rude and violent sort of law is pernicious; but there is another which La Fontaine calls "the good natural law." This law of nature teaches us pleasure,

pleasure in the sense in which La Fontaine extols it, that is to say, that wholesome and exquisite type of pleasure that gives keen and profitable delight to soul and body alike: conversation, reading, "diverting thoughts," a fine dwelling, beautiful paintings, splendid gardens; and it is not forbidden to add to such pleasures as these (but in moderation) good wine and fair women.

The great master of this "free thought" is Saint-Evremond. From 1661 Saint-Evremond lives in London in dignified and cheerful exile. But it seems that his prestige is enhanced by his absence. There is the utmost eagerness to procure everything that he prints or, rather, permits to be printed, and that enters France through open or secret channels. Whether he discusses Corneille or Racine, the diverse characteristics of the Roman people, or the skepticism of the maréchal d'Hocquincourt, his alert and sprightly style enthralls his readers. His rationalism delights: not an imperious rationalism but a refined and inquisitive rationalism that penetrates all the essential mysteries of things and dissipates alike the prestige of dogma and the lies of the commandments. And there is a tendency to indulge with Saint-Evremond in what is "natural":

in the pleasures of thinking freely, of enjoying beautiful things, of making of life not a bitter struggle but an elegant compromise.

The school of Saint-Evremond naturally had the most disciples of all; it was the easiest to follow. But after 1660, and particularly after 1680, there was a more austere and "philosophical" type of "free thought." It was defended by Gabriel Naudé, by Gassendi, and without doubt by Molière; they found their inspiration in Epicurus. This philosophy, which is quite prudent, does not clash with Christian belief. We do not find genuine audacity in such matters before Bayle and Fontenelle. But even then "audacity" is merely the exercise of Cartesian reason, that spirit of free criticism that Bossuet rightly feared: "I see a great combat being prepared against the Church under the name of Cartesian philosophy. There is being introduced, with this philosophy as a pretext, a certain liberty of judgment by virtue of which one may boldly assert whatever one thinks, without concern for tradition." Bossuet fears for dogmatic Tradition. Bayle feigns to respect it; but he claims for himself the liberty to judge that particular type of tradition that is written with a small letter: tradition, or rather, traditions.

He publishes his *Thoughts on the Comet*, a work which discusses the opinion that comets presage terrible misfortunes. In the course of this discussion one comes upon other traditions which are also perhaps mere phantasms. For example, it has long been maintained that religion is true, were it only because it is necessary; destroy it and all society will crumble in disastrous chaos. All this is a mere hypothesis, quite erroneous in fact, says Bayle; and he proves that a society composed of atheists might very well exist and prosper.

Even if one disregards these very serious and dangerous problems that involve religion, history is full of hypotheses that tradition transmits without discussion and that reason has the right to examine. To solve a certain number of the problems involved, Bayle compiles his voluminous *Dictionary*. It is a monument of erudition; but it hardly interests us any longer. The people whose history Bayle writes are, for the most part, so obscure that it really matters little whether what is said about them be accurate or not. Yet the *Dictionary* was perhaps the greatest work of the first half of the eighteenth century. In the catalogues of 500 private libraries I found this work included most frequently (288 times). The fact is that Bayle (and without doubt his readers) is less interested in the problems themselves than in the method that is employed to discuss them. A prudent method it is, and the conclusions in the articles themselves are orthodox; but in the notes Bayle rigorously applies the rules of historical criticism. Here we find comparisons, discussion of evidence, textual examination; all sorts of pretended truths are relegated to the status of fables, and when the occasion calls for it—which is quite often— Bayle is as merciless to Christian truths, including miracles, lives of the saints, and falsified or forged texts.

Fontenelle reasoned much as Bayle did and reached the same conclusions. He wrote a *History of the Oracles* to demonstrate that oracles never predicted anything and that they took advantage of human credulity. Yet, even very intelligent people had believed in oracles. Abundant and precise proof had been given of their veracity; at least the proof was considered to be precise. Fontenelle shows what is concealed behind this apparent accuracy. There follows a rigorous criticism of errors of opinion; it is perfectly possible to find these same errors in all religious opinions. A slight transition, and then Fontenelle leads his reader from the criticism of paganism to an examination of Christianity. To his critical spirit Fontenelle also adds the scientific spirit. The sciences were beginning to enjoy great esteem after 1630 and particularly after 1690. Their progress was extolled; and Perrault made them an essential argument in the *Quarrel of the Ancients and the Moderns*. Now the progress of the sciences was that of human intelligence. Man was not merely a fallen creature, devoted to sin, expiation, and self-sacrifice. He could create, conquer, dominate nature. Reason, or at least a certain type of reason, revealed to him immense horizons of activity and hope.

This species of reason, indeed, was prudent and modest. For, after all, the sciences at the same time that they magnify man render him insignificant. "Man is only a point in nature," said Pascal; yet Pascal thought that the earth was in the center of the universe. Fontenelle teaches the plurality of worlds, the system of Copernicus. The earth is only a planet and a very small one, to boot. Like man himself, it is lost in the infinite. Let us cease believing therefore that the world was made for us, that God has to busy himself with us only. Let us imitate those scientists whose praises Fontenelle is never weary of singing. Let us observe facts; let us submit them to precise experimentation. Let us endeavor to know nature, not metaphysical nature, the *natura naturans* and *the natura naturata* of the Scholastics, but that which is before our eyes, that of the physicist, the chemist, the naturalist.

The wide extent of this philosophical movement is indicated by the abundance of works, translations, and readers. Men like the marquis de Lassay or Raymond le Grec extol "lay morality," the morality of nature in the best sense of the term, the morality of temperate and selected pleasure. Likewise, in many scholars we find critical curiosity combined with historical skepticism. We find this curiosity and skepticism in the accounts of imaginary voyages and Utopias which multiply at the end of the seventeenth century and the beginning of the eighteenth. The *Austral Land* of G. de Foigny (1676), the *History of the Sevarambes,* by Denis Veiras (1677), the *Voyages and Adventures of Jacques Massé* by Tyssot de Patot (1710), the *History of the Isle of Calejava, or the Isle of Rational Men* by A. Gilbert (1700)—these are not illustrious

works, but they are read, and almost all enjoy
a second edition. They are not mere tales of
adventure. They are really rational "parallels"
between our traditional political and religious
beliefs and the politics or religion that rationalism might conceive. Now what reason
constructs is quite different from our traditions: we find that it gives us natural religion,
equality, or even communism.

This spirit of innovation is strengthened by
the reading and translation of a great number
of English works. Erudites and scholars read
the *Philosophical Transactions of the Royal
Society of London*. Almost all of Locke is
translated before 1700: his *Education of Children*, his *Reasonable Christianity*, his *Letter
on Tolerance,* then his *Essay on Human Understanding.* Translations are also made of the
works of many moralists and deistic theologians (Clifford, Sherlock, Collins, Clarke, Ad-
dison, Pope). Newspapers are founded, the
very titles of which indicate that they are especially interested in English matters (*The English Library,* 1717-1728, *The Literary Memoirs of Great Britain,* 1720-1724, *The British
Library,* 1733-1747). *Gulliver's Travels* is
translated in 1727. After 1720, and more definitely after 1730, England becomes the coun-

try of political liberty and of freedom of thought, and in those particulars—so it is affirmed or inferred—a model for Frenchmen to follow.

CHAPTER II

RATIONALISTIC OPTIMISM
AND ITS CONSEQUENCES

Historical note.—Voltaire,[1] irritable and vain, soon quarreled with Frederick II. He was compelled to leave Prussia rather ingloriously in 1753 and to establish himself in Switzerland in 1754. He had published the *Century of Louis XIV* (1751), the tale of *Micromégas* (1752), the poem of the *Natural Law* (1756), the important *Essay on the Customs and the Spirit of Nations* (1756), the tale of *Candide* (1759). Ferney soon became a place of pilgrimage for numerous visitors. The celebrity of Voltaire was increased by his efforts in behalf of various victims of intolerance: the Protestant, Calas, broken on the wheel, on the false accusation of having killed his son, who was on the point of becoming a Catholic; the Protestant, Sirven, accused of having drowned his daughter, who was a Catholic; the chevalier de la Barre, decapitated because he had not doffed his hat as a procession passed by, and also because he was accused of having mutilated a crucifix. In 1778 Voltaire returned to Paris, where he was greeted with the wildest enthusiasm. At Ferney he had written with ceaseless activity mediocre tragedies, witty poems, tales (*The Ingenuous Man,* 1767), historical and philosophical works (*Treatise on*

---

[1] For the first part of the life of Voltaire, cf. p. 3.

52

Tolerance, 1763; a small *Philosophical Dictionary,* 1764; *Questions Concerning the Encyclopedia,* 1770); and a vast number of pamphlets and tracts of religious polemics (*Sermon of the Fifty,* 1762; *An Important Analysis by Mylord Bolingbroke,* 1765).

The principal philosophers were:

The abbé de Condillac (1714-1780), who led a studious and simple life and was on terms of intimacy with the leading philosophers. His works are the *Essay on the Origin of Human Knowledge* (1746), the *Treatise on Systems* (1749), and the *Treatise on Sensations* (1754).

Helvétius (1715-1771), a very wealthy farmer-general, whose salon was the rendezvous of philosophers. His book *Of the Mind* appeared in 1758. The *Treatise on Man* was published in 1772 after his death.

D'Holbach (1723-1789), who was also very wealthy and who became the "major-domo of philosophy." He wrote, undoubtedly in collaboration with Diderot, *Natural Politics* (1773), *The Social System* (1773) and works of religious polemics (*Christianity Exposed,* 1761; *The System of Nature,* 1770).

D'Alembert (1717-1783), the natural son of Mme Tencin; as permanent secretary of the French Academy (1771) he exercised considerable influence. Besides the preliminary discourse of the *Encyclopedia* and certain learned mathematical treatises, he composed many short literary works which were decidedly mediocre.

The abbé Raynal published in 1770 a vast *Philosophical and Political History of the Establishments and the Commerce of Europeans in the Two Indies.* With the collaboration of Diderot, d'Holbach, and others, he published two greatly augmented editions of the work (1774, 1780), in which he developed his attacks upon fanaticism and in which he made a vigorous humanitarian appeal.

The abbé de Mably (1709-1785) at first dabbled in

politics, as the secretary of the cardinal de Tencin. Then he published a great number of works on political philosophy (*Observations on the History of France*, 1765; *Of Legislation or the Principle of Laws,* 1776; *Observations on the Government of the United States of America,* 1784.)

Condorcet (1743-1794) wrote, before the Revolution, a certain number of treatises on mathematics and political economy, a life of Turgot (1786), a life of Voltaire (1787). A member of the Legislative Assembly of the Convention, he was arrested as a Girondin and took poison while awaiting trial.

Finally we must cite certain works which, for all their mediocrity, enjoyed great success and influence in the eighteenth century:

Boulanger, *Antiquity Revealed* (1766)—Delisle de Sales, *The Philosophy of Nature* (1770)—Morelly, *The Code of Nature* (1755)—Guillard de Beaurieu, *The Pupil of Nature* (1763).

For Montesquieu, cf. p. 101; Diderot, p. 149; the *Encyclopedia*, p. 150; J.-J. Rousseau, p. 187.

General principles.—The first principle of the philosophers is a carefully reasoned optimism. They no longer believe that the earth is a vale of tears and that all human effort should be directed toward the task of subduing one's corrupt nature in order to avoid sin; their philosophy, which continues that of Molière, La Fontaine, and Saint-Evremond, teaches that life is intrinsically good if one arrange it rationally. This joy in living takes the form of a rather unlovely egotism and a mere desire for sensual pleasure, in the *Worldly Man* of Voltaire (1736). All is well, because Voltaire and his friends have fine clothes, fine carriages, good suppers, and the rest. But Voltaire's optimism is not entirely sensual; it is also due to the fact that beautiful tragedies and beautiful paintings are constantly coming into being. The Englishman, Mandeville, in his *Fable of the Bees* (translated in 1740) and the Frenchman, Melon, demonstrated that pleasure, luxury, good suppers, and the rest, all have their utility. Through them industry prospers and commerce is developed. The joy of some saves others from poverty. Yet after all poverty does exist; and experience proves that one is never certain of supping well and living well. For there is sickness and injustice, there is persecution and war. Even when one is a Voltaire, one is not always pampered by a marquise de Châtelet and protected by a Mme de Pompadour. The marquise deceives you and Mme de Pompadour abandons you. Besides, one is ill. One must leave France and then Prussia. Consequently the joyous *Worldly Man* tempers his good humor rather quickly. His optimism, like that of Montesquieu, Buffon, and others, is hardly anything more than prudence and resignation.

But this uneasy skepticism is always tempered by one very definite hope. The world as it is, thinks Voltaire, functions but indifferently or even badly. But if to-day we have misery, despotism, fanaticism, folly, the world of to-morrow can and should function more perfectly. Candide, after having sounded the depths of human despair, still has the courage to "cultivate his garden." That is because, in spite of everything, he has faith in the future. At present "all men are equally mad" (Voltaire says so again and again), and the opinion that governs the world is the opinion of diseased minds or imbeciles; but after a time this opinion will be directed by the wise. Little by little, intelligence will triumph over ignorance, and reason over prejudice, injustice, and violence.

There is justification, therefore, in rejoicing at the "conquests of reason" and in having faith in these conquests. Now, to prepare the future one must appeal to reason. The *Encyclopedia* is a "reasoned" dictionary of human knowledge, the inventory of whatever reason has set down, corrected, prepared. All great literary works up to 1760, almost all after that date (excluding sentimental literature), are "reasoned" and rational works. The *Persian*

Letters oppose the reason of a Persian, that is to say, of a rational Parisian, to the lack of reason of the Parisians in general. The *Spirit of the Laws* seeks the rational element underlying all law. The *Philosophical Letters* are never merely a traveler's picturesque tale; they constitute the study of English reason. The tales of Voltaire represent the clash of reason with the lack of reason, of fortune, or of men; the *Henriade* constitutes a defense of the first monarch of whom it could be said that he was "reasonable."

However, we should carefully define this word "reason." It is not the scholastic reason that borrows its truths, even its incomprehensible truths, from Aristotle or Saint Thomas, and that rationally deducts the consequences; it is on the contrary Cartesian, mathematical reason. Until about 1750, to reason implies to start with principles that are evident to everybody, or that one considers to be evident, and then to proceed from one inevitable consequence to another; one thinks as does a mathematician or a "geometrician." The very enemies of this "geometry," as well as its friends, recognize that it hardly has had a serious rival. Says the abbé Dubos: "It is the vaunted art of synthesis based upon sound de-duction." To be sure, Duclos observes that "geometry, which has succeeded erudition, is beginning to be unfashionable"; and Diderot in his *Thoughts on the Interpretation of Nature* foresees a "great revolution in the sciences," which will dethrone geometry. But nevertheless, all the notable philosophers have studied and even diligently cultivated mathematics: Fontenelle, Voltaire, Montesquieu, Diderot, J.-J. Rousseau, Condillac. D'Alembert was an illustrious geometrician before becoming a noted philosopher.

The certitude of geometry, however, presents a certain amount of incertitude: for its first truths are axioms which cannot be demonstrated, but which are purely arbitrary. The geometrical method in philosophy also had its dangers and its postulates. These postulates are summed up in the affirmation that what is evident to the reason of Voltaire, d'Alembert, Condillac, and Condorcet is evident to the men of every country and every era, and that the consequences deduced therefrom ought naturally to be evident to street-porters as well as to Academicians, to Iroquois as well as to Frenchmen. It was believed after Descartes that "common sense" sufficed and that "common sense" was the most bountifully

shared entity in the world. Men began, therefore, to construct arguments based upon "common sense." For example, in order to know
man, in order to know the formation and the
nature of his thought, they no longer consulted
Aristotle, Saint Paul, or Saint Thomas. They
relied upon "reasoning." Condillac postulates
a statue exactly as the mathematician postulates mass and movement. He postulates a
sense, and reasons upon the impressions that
the statue receives from this sense; then he
postulates a second sense, and so on. This type
of hypothesis and this method of reasoning are
current throughout the eighteenth century:
one finds them in Buffon and in the Genevan
philosopher, Bonnet. Or else they are improved upon. Instead of a statue, one
postulates a child whom one supposes to be
without heredity and temperament; he is to
be brought up in a cavern or a cage (according to La Mettrie, Delisle de Sales, Guillard
de Beaurieu). And one imagines, *a priori,* all
sorts of experiences and the consequences of
these experiences. Or else, as in the case of
Helvétius, one postulates a human mind that
one declares to be identical in all men at birth,
ready to submit in identical fashion to the same
impressions; and one reasons geometrically

upon the different results of different impressions. This philosophical geometry possesses a certain invincible fascination. Even economists who study the realities of grain, cattle, and commerce, and who, moreover, know of these by experience believe that economic truths are susceptible of mathematical demonstration, that they are universal and absolute.

It is obvious that this method of reasoning is quite worthless in the sciences that are based upon observation, as Voltaire ascertained to his cost. He desired, counter to the observations of Buffon, to reason about the origin of fossils, and he came to the conclusion that they had fallen from the cloaks of pilgrims or that they germinated in the ground. But whither did this method lead, or rather, whither would it have led, had the philosophers known of no other in solving the problems of destiny, history, and social life?

The consequences: natural religion and tolerance.—It led first of all to religious discussion. Religion was still, as at the time of La Bruyère, one of those "sublime topics" which it was not vouchsafed the profane to discuss. But there was deserved indignation at the forbidding. "One is not satisfied with the probable in scientific matters: one requires demonstration; why should one content one-self with the probable in religion? Every religion boasts that it is the true religion; in order to be able to choose among these various creeds one should be convinced by clear and evident proof. If existing religions cannot present any, we must seek a religion that can; if I deliberately blindfold my eyes, how shall I find it?" (*An Examination into the Nature of Religion, Attributed to M. de Saint-Evremond.*) Diderot, or the pseudo Saint-Evremond, makes statements like these in manuscripts that he does not publish or in books that circulate secretly. But one may suggest, even if one does not affirm. The *Encyclopedia,* bolder than the *Dictionary* of Bayle, indicates all the religious problems that should be determined by reason and not by authority. The articles on the *Bible, Christianity, Infernal Punishments,* and many others rely upon the Church for the ultimate decision on the problems that are presented. But they begin by slyly presenting all these problems and the difficulties that they entail. Gradually two doctrines are disseminated, and one of them really becomes the dominant opinion among the cultivated classes.

It is deism or "natural religion." There is

indeed, it is maintained, a certain divine element in Christianity; but so there is in Buddhism or Mohammedanism, so there is in the creed of the Parsees, or the Incas, or the Algonquins. When one prunes the diverse and sundry religions of absurdities, contradictions, and the inventions of priests, there remain certain common beliefs. These are true because they are common to all faiths and because they satisfy reason, or at least do not run counter to it. There is a God, who is not confused with the world that He has created; He has given man conscience, the faculty of distinguishing between good and evil; He has given him a soul which is assuredly—or without much doubt—or perhaps—immortal, and which will be punished for its faults and rewarded for its virtues. This deism is the religion of Montesquieu, Voltaire, the marquis d'Argens, Duclos, Toussaint, d'Alembert, Mably, Condorcet, in fact almost all the philosophers and their devotees. They are at variance only with respect to the "assuredly, without much doubt, perhaps" of the immortal soul. Montesquieu, d'Alembert, and Duclos favor certitude, at least publicly. Voltaire says "Yes," then "Perhaps," then "No." Yet to the very end he shrinks from materialism.

There were indeed few materialists and most of them kept their negations to themselves. They reasoned thus: There is only one element in the world, and that is matter. It is God, if you will, for it is everything. This matter is more or less highly organized. It may have life and feeling: it may be a plant or an animal; it may have thought: it may be man. At death the elements of human matter are dispersed, as are all other elements. This materialism is suggested, not very openly though, in the works of Helvétius. D'Holbach devotes a whole chapter to the negation of the spirituality of the soul. There are other atheists: Fontenelle, the abbé de Saint-Pierre, Barbeyrac, Boulanger (if one is to believe Voltaire); more certainly Deslandes, Morelly; most assuredly Fréret, the curate Meslier, Naigeon, Sylvain Maréchal. But there are really only two important atheists: La Mettrie (*The Man-Plant, The Man-Machine*) and especially Diderot.

Diderot did not seek notoriety. In his published works he suggests materialism; he never affirms it. But it was he who made of this materialism something more than a mere blustering negation; he really created experimental materialism. In denying the spirituality of the soul and consequently its immortality, its very existence even, he does not reason, for reasoning in matters such as these follows one's heart's desire. Diderot observes; he experiments. He observes that the soul is bound to the body by such indissoluble ties that one cannot sharply delimit the province of soul or body. He observes that our moral temperament is only the reflection of our physical temperament; that if our bodies are affected by sickness, poison, hypnotism, somnambulism, our souls are affected to the same extent. The bonds which unite body and soul are therefore so inseparable from the experimental point of view that thought and matter are only one and the same thing. "The peasant who sees a watch functioning and who, ignorant of its mechanism, identifies each hand with a spirit is neither more nor less stupid than our spiritualists."

Diderot kept most of these affirmations to himself or, at most, set them down in manuscript form; consequently they had no influence. But deists and atheists alike agreed in two doctrines that had a considerable rôle in molding public opinion.

The first is that if "natural religion" is "natural," all the various dogmatic beliefs are errors and illusions. The philosophers refuse to admit that one may believe, unless indeed one be an imbecile, what seems absurd to reason. Consequently the history of religions ought to indicate, as indeed it *does* indicate, the same sequence of events in the case of every religion. There exists in the ignorant and wretched mob an invincible fear and the concomitant instinct for appeasing mysterious and fearful powers. Adroit rogues have exploited this fear. They have invented gods and the obscure and terrible commandments of these gods. They have called themselves the intermediaries between human weakness and divine power. They have caused themselves to be feared and they have set a high price for their intervention. At the same time they have been wont to associate themselves with despots who have supported them with force of arms, and whom they, in turn, have invested with mystic prestige. The history of religions, then, is the history of knavery, of exploitation, of tyranny.

Even if men do not dare to say openly that religion is false, they vehemently demand tolerance. This doctrine of tolerance was very slow in attaining formulation. Most of the good people of the seventeenth century approved of the revocation of the Edict of

Nantes. In serene and even jovial mood, Fénelon betook himself to Saintonge to superintend the application of the most odious measures of enforcement. Even the skeptics, including "freethinkers" like Saint-Evremond, are inclined to blame the stubborn Protestants for everything. But, little by little, violence in religious matters becomes less prevalent; the family quarrels of Quietism and Jansenism have brought about a reaction. One can discuss tolerance and publicly defend it. Bayle does so; even Fénelon, later in life, is not hostile. One reads the English theologians, like Locke and Collins, who combat every form of persecution. The *Persian Letters* and the *Spirit of the Laws* of Montesquieu, the *Chinese Letters* of d'Argens, the tales of Voltaire (*The Travels of Scarmentado, Zadig, Micromégas,* and so forth) effectively employ irony and sarcasm in inveighing against intolerance. Toward 1750 the cause of tolerance has admittedly gained the day. In the Sorbonne students of theology, Turgot, the abbé de Brienne, the abbé Morellet, discuss tolerance and decide in favor of it. One may even attack intolerance with the royal approbation and authorization. The article on *Gomarists* in the *Encyclopedia* (by Morellet) is not very considerate of the authorities who claim the right to impose beliefs by imprisonment, the galleys, or the gibbet. After 1760 intolerance still has a few defenders; but their timid voices are lost amid general cries of indignation. The Calas affair, the Sirven affair, the la Barre affair, utterly discredit fanaticism. Delisle de Sales calculates with splendid precision that since the beginning of the world fanaticism has caused the death of 33,095,290 human beings; and Raynal, whose eloquent periods are suggested or even dictated by Diderot, makes the *History of the Two Indies* a history of Catholic cruelties in the two Indies.

It is easy to point out the unjust acts of which the philosophers were guilty in the battle, and the unpleasantly acrimonious character of their polemics. Let us merely recall that there were certain extenuating circumstances. For a long time the defenders of Christianity had argued on no higher plane than their adversaries. Besides, these defenders could have their adversaries hanged; they *did* send them to the galleys. And the partisans of intolerance, from time to time, cast the Protestants into prison, put their daughters into Catholic convents, or hanged their ministers. The philosophers were guilty of something else besides mere violence of language, or rather, they were guilty of a more unmistakable sort of error.

They had practically no understanding of the essential character of the religious spirit or of faith. They were not wrong in denouncing forced conversions and the alliance that had placed the punitive resources of the temporal power at the disposal of the spiritual power. But they were incapable of understanding that one might believe in certain truths that were not "reasonable" without necessarily being either a rogue or a dupe. They never wished to admit the reasons that reason itself does not comprehend and the intuitive certainty that sets little store by the control of history and the observations of the naturalists. It was for that reason that they were guilty of such stupid utterances whenever they spoke of what Auguste Comte calls "the theological epochs," whenever they discussed the great men whose grandeur is of a mystic order. Voltaire, Mably, Condorcet, and the rest never cared to see in the crusades (following the abbé Fleury in this respect) anything but wars of adventure and of gross cupidity; Voltaire, d'Argens, and Helvétius spoke of the great mystics and, among others, of St. Francis of Assisi as ridiculous fools; Voltaire dealt with Joan of Arc in a mock epic, the *Virgin Maid,* that is a masterpiece of coarse stupidity. The serious thing about it all is that the work caused a scandal not because of the subject matter but because of the obscenity of its treatment. As a matter of fact, the *Virgin Maid* was quite popular. Joan of Arc was not a "reasonable" heroine; precisely for that reason nobody understood her, at least not before 1770.

Natural or lay morality.—If one denies revealed religion and if one keeps only a vague sort of "natural religion," what is to become of morality? Until now morality had been only one of the names of religion. If one wished to live uprightly, one consulted neither one's conscience nor one's principles but the commandments of God and the Church. And if one were embarrassed, one consulted not one's reason but one's confessor or one's spiritual director. The philosophers might very well have disregarded this particular problem: "Let us seek truth and let morality fare as best it can!" But they all tried to save morality while freeing it from religion.

The attempt had already been made long before. Very often indeed there had been an instinctive tendency, if not to organize an independent code of morals, at least to speak of morality as if it were self-sufficient. The greater part of the *Characters* of La Bruyère, who was a devout Christian, might well have been written by a freethinker. The taste for moralizing grows as philosophy progresses. Some three hundred works bearing on morality had been published within fifty years before La Bruyère's time, but in the following period even a greater number were published within twenty-five years; and in these *Thoughts, Reflections,* and *Characters,* religion has a constantly diminishing rôle. As we have already observed, Bayle states the problem bluntly in a chapter heading of the *Thoughts on the Comet:* "Atheism is not necessarily conducive to the corruption of morals. Conjectures [very favorable ones they are, too] concerning the morals of a society existing without religion." These chapters created a scandal. But his opinion, which at first was considered so scandalous, was soon shared by everybody. In the *Telemachus* of Fénelon, in the *Cyrus* of Ramsay and the *Sethos* of Terrasson, which imitate *Telemachus,* it is the pagans who are virtuous. Explicitly, all the philosophers believe in a morality that is self-sufficient, men like Montesquieu in the *Persian Letters,* Voltaire in his *Treatise on Metaphysics* (1734), his tales, his *Discourses in Verse on Man* (1734-1737), his *Poem on the Natural Law* (1756), to say nothing of the first less famous philosophers, d'Argens, Deslandes, Barbeyrac, and others. They take their stand, however, with a certain amount of moderation, not stressing the fact that this natural morality is independent of religious morality. It was the lawyer, Toussaint, who took the first bold step in that famous book of his, *Morals* (1748), which created indignation and which was condemned, but which went through at least twenty editions before the Revolution. "What is virtue? It is constant fidelity in fulfilling the obligations that *reason* dictates to us." And this "reason" has nothing to do with religion. "Religion is concerned in the matter only in so far as it tends to inculcate morals; now, inasmuch as natural reason suffices for that purpose, I need say no more. . . . This work of mine is intended for Mohammedans as well as for Christians."

Toussaint had much the same experience as Bayle. Soon everybody was openly in his favor: Duclos ("Religion represents the perfection and not the basis of morality"), d'Alembert, all those who belonged to the "philosophical" party, and many others. Even materialists like Helvétius, d'Holbach, Diderot, and Naigeon shared his viewpoint. These materialists had a more difficult task in this affair. They were obliged to deny the existence of liberty at the same time that they denied God and the soul. After all, if we are not free, how can one speak to us of duty? One does not teach a watch to keep exact time through an appeal to its conscience. But all the materialists are more insistent upon morality than they are upon their materialism. In order not to be embarrassed at the contradiction involved, they ignore it, or feign to ignore it. "Virtue," says La Mettrie, "can take very deep root in the atheist, whereas it often clings by a thread, so to speak, to the surface of a pious heart." D'Holbach devotes a part of his books to the teaching of morality and an entire chapter to the proof of the statement that "atheism is compatible with morality." As for Diderot, if he reasons most ardently about materialism, he teaches morality with pathetic supplication, with "trembling," and with "tears." Truth is a "great monument" but virtue is another monument "erected upon the surface of the earth."

It was not sufficient to postulate the principle of natural morality; it was necessary to justify it. Religious morality is justified by religion. It is a direct commandment of God, dictated by God, interpreted by His ministers. In natural morality, however, there is no longer any revealed law. One must put something in its place; and at first this "something" was "moral instinct."

Man has a desire for good and an aversion for evil, just as he has belief in God, love of life, and fear of death. It is an innate idea; or at least, its germ is innate. Locke did not believe in this innateness of morality any more than did Montaigne. But such is the doctrine of the English poet, Pope, in those *Essays on Man* (1730) the translations of which went through at least twenty editions in twenty years. Voltaire, although he hesitates and contradicts himself in this matter as in others, almost always defends this point of view. "God has given man the ideas of justice and conscience" (first part of the *Poem on the Natural Law*). "Morality is the same in the case of all civilized nations" (*Preface* of the *Essay on Customs*). Finally even the more audacious philosophers, Morelly, Delisle de

Sales, and Mably have this same belief in innate morality.

Still, the hypothesis of "innate" moral ideas is among those that perplex our philosophers. It resembles too closely those ideas of Descartes which one no longer fancies; and it contradicts Locke, in whom one believes. There is consequently an attempt to justify morality in the same way that one explains the faculties of the mind. One can no more speak of an innate idea or instinct than one can of innate memory or reasoning. Morality is born of the interplay of sensations and impressions. Man lives; he lives in society. The attempts at social organization reveal to him the necessity of permanent rules which are to be superior to the whims of individuals. Egotistic instinct observes that it has every reason to respect a part of the instincts of the rest. Morality thus represents social experience. It is the doctrine of La Mettrie. It is, above all, the doctrine that Helvétius does not openly express, but that is suggested throughout his book, *Of the Mind*. Originally all minds are similar and similarly egotistic; it is education, the fruit of the practical experience of generations, that develops in the mind moral sentiments, born of practice, and meant to serve practically. This doctrine should also have been adopted by Diderot and d'Holbach, for it is the only one that is in accordance with their materialism. It tempts them; they approach it; they develop it implicitly or parenthetically. But its barrenness disturbs them; Helvétius finds himself opposed to Diderot, as well as to Voltaire and J.-J. Rousseau.

However that may be, the partisans of moral instinct and those of experimental morality are in agreement in two essential doctrines.

The first is that if morality is a rule, it should not be a source of restraint. The "maréchale" of Diderot asks whether it be not the essential characteristic of religion to run counter to this wretchedly corrupt nature of ours. Natural morality endeavors on the contrary to contradict as little as possible. The philosophers take up again and render more precise the arguments of Saint-Evremond and Fontenelle, which they find again in the English deists. "Virtue is not a thing that should burden us," says Montesquieu (*Persian Letters*).

He told me, "Be happy"; and that quite sufficed:

that is the teaching of the *Discourses* of Voltaire *On Man,* and these discourses utterly refute the Jansenists and the Stoics. Morelly, La Mettrie, Maupertuis, Toussaint, Diderot, Delisle de Sales intend to establish the reign of happiness as well as that of morality. Happiness is "the sovereign goal of life" (Maupertuis). "To enjoy," says Saint-Lambert,

"To enjoy is to honor God; He bids us be gay."

It will be easy to reconcile enjoyment and virtue as soon as it is understood that morality need not enter the lists against the so-called corrupt passions. On the contrary it must admit that these passions are good in themselves when one does not substitute artificial passions for the natural passions. This rehabilitation of the passions is the common theme of almost all the philosophers, and of a great number of moralists who are not philosophers, or who are only partly so. One finds it in Lemaître de Claville (*Treatise on Real Merit in Man,* 1734); in Levesque de Pouilly (*Theory of Agreeable Sentiments,* 1736) ; more clearly in Vauvenargues, Duclos, Toussaint, Helvétius, Diderot, d'Holbach, Naigeon, Delisle de Sales, and many others.

The second point is that morality can be only a social morality. Certainly my passions are "good, useful, and agreeable" for me, and I never act more ardently than when I obey them. But those of my neighbor are also good for him. It behooves me, then, to come to an agreement with my neighbor; and morality is precisely the science of this agreement. It is a science which might become complicated perhaps, if it were not so easy, according to the philosophers, to teach that the most agreeable passion of all is to forget one's own interests in serving those of others: the most certain form of enjoyment is that of "humanity." The *Seventh Discourse* of Voltaire *On Man:* "Virtue consists of doing good to one's fellow men and not of indulging in vain practices of mortification." The third part of the *Morals* of Toussaint is devoted to the "social virtues." "Let the legislature," concludes Mably, "decree that young citizens be taught to judge of the degree of goodness or badness of an action by the advantage or detriment that will accrue to others." The *Universal Catechism* of Saint-Lambert insists upon one's duties toward men in general—toward one's fatherland—toward one's family. That was the catechism of all the philosophers, Turgot, Morellet, Morelly, De-

lisle de Sales, L.-S. Mercier, Raynal; it was
also that of the materialists, La Mettrie,
Helvétius, d'Holbach, and Diderot.

Rational politics.—At the same time that it
discussed the problems of religion and morality, philosophical thought boldly attacked
that other all-important topic: politics. In
truth, necessity had impelled men to discuss
the matter since the end of Louis XIV's reign.
Political affairs were going so badly, not only
for those subject to the *taille* and the *corvée*
but even for the members of the privileged
classes, that people began to doubt the perfection of existing political principles. Fénelon,
in certain writings of his which were not published, in his *Telemachus* which *was* published, Boisguilbert in his *Existing Situation
in France* (1695), Vauban in his *Royal Tithe,*
Boulainvilliers in his *Condition of France*
(1727), did not discuss the monarchical idea
nor even absolute monarchy. But they did
wish that this monarchy might provide itself
with states-general or parliaments or at least
more judicious and humane councilors and
methods. Men were beginning to make comparisons. After having conceived a horror of
England, which had decapitated a king and
brought about a religious revolution, they be-

gan to wonder if England's *Magna Charta*
and her Parliament, if her political liberty
and freedom of thought were not the cause of
her prosperity. Between 1700 and 1730 there
is an ever increasing interest in England's political writers as well as her theologians. At
last people are beginning to "examine principles." That "reason" which dares to subject
to its sway the problems of the cycloid, of the
mercury tube, of the fall of bodies, or of the
origin of ideas very soon takes it upon itself to
inquire into the origin of political ideas and
the motives that condemn or justify them.
This examination is romantic in the case of
the Utopias of which we have spoken, which
fashioned the socialistic or communistic constitutions of the Sevarambes or of the Austral
Land; it becomes austerely methodical in the
translated works of Grotius (1677; translated by Barbeyrac, 1724) and Puffendorf
(translated by Barbeyrac, 1706); the translator, Barbeyrac, comments on the ideas in question with audacious clarity. Discussion begins
to pass timidly from the library and the study
to the world of action. Some politically
minded souls meet in the *Club of the Entresol* [2]

[2] [The meetings of the Club were held at the residence of the
abbé Alary, in the *entresol* of a house in the place Vendôme
(Paris): hence the name.]

(1724-1731) to discuss the public welfare, government, and law. And these timid and private discussions already seem so audacious that the authorities become uneasy and the club is closed.

Little by little, men's spirits are emboldened. The *English Letters* of Voltaire give a lengthy description of the functioning of the English constitution, the check exercised by Parliament, the vote on taxation, the liberty of thinking and writing about state as well as religious matters. The *Persian Letters* of Montesquieu discuss public rights, the rights of the people, depopulation. The *Spirit of the Laws* boldly examines all the different constitutions and decides that the best is that in which the various powers are set off against each other, in which monarchical authority is limited by the rights and liberties of citizens. One may say that after 1750, and particularly after 1760, provided that it mask its bold sallies under allusions and abstract generalities, philosophy can discuss politics freely.

Therein it employs "philosophical" methods which in certain respects differ radically from our modern methods. For us, politics should be as much as possible an experimental science or at least a science based upon realities. The science of government seems to us quite different from that of geometry; one must have something besides axioms, theorems, and corollaries. It can act upon life only on condition that it take life itself as its point of departure. Political science can find this "life" in history, in the examples of the past, in the analysis of fortunate or unhappy experiences of a race or of a people. Above all, if one mistrusts "lessons from history," there are economic facts, the precise realities of births and deaths, of the grain that one harvests, of the cloth that one manufactures, of the ships that import or export. Now the political writers of the eighteenth century have but a confused idea of these two methods.

History does not exist as yet, or rather, it is only beginning to be organized. Voltaire and a few others create modern history, as we shall see. They make of history not the glorification of a king, of a dynasty, or of a few exalted figures, but the history of a generation or of several generations. They demand that history be not merely eloquent or diverting, but that it be exact above all things. But Voltaire and all the others had not always the historical sense. They understood well enough that the king was not the nation, that a congress of

diplomats did not enable us to analyze the
habits of a shopkeeper or the rebellious impulses of a peasant. But they did not fully understand that a shopkeeper of Bagdad was not
a shopkeeper of the Marais and that a peasant
of the period of the crusades was not obedient
or rebellious for the same reasons as a Round-
head of Cromwell or a farmer-subject of Louis
XV. Voltaire judges the acts of a feudal baron
or a Chinese mandarin as he does those of a
Fleury or a Turgot. He ascribes to a soldier
of the crusades the same mercenary motives
that he does to a recruit of the Seven Years'
War. When Mably seeks the principles of just
and happy societies he does not realize that
justice may represent a changing ideal and
that various peoples may have very different
and mutually irreconcilable ways of being
happy. In the empyrean his soul is represented
as meeting those of all the great legislators:
he "seeks the approbation of Plato"; he con-
verses "with Cicero at Tusculum." But neither
Plato nor Cicero conceived of the historical
method in politics. Valid economic methods
were even more difficult to follow in the eighteenth century. Economic realities were still in
large part unknown. Moreover, France was
infinitely variegated and what was true for

one province might be erroneous for a neighboring province. Methodical information was hardly available until after 1760, and such information as there was would not have been sufficient to justify general conclusions. Political writers, therefore, had to seek other methods.

The psychological method and the natural method.—The first was the method that had enabled one to best understand the fundamental element of human society, man. Nothing but vain systems had been set up to explain the nature of man and the mind of man as long as one did not proceed from the simple to the compound, as long as one did not discern what was primitive and what was only a transformation of primitive elements. Locke and Condillac start with the sensations and show how they engender attention, memory, judgment, and so forth. In the same way, human society represents a group of men who have combined in order to satisfy the elementary needs of commercial life. These needs are genuine enough, since neither hares nor lions live in society and since man might have lived in isolation as they do. The task of the philosopher therefore will be to segregate in the human mind—in all its manifestations in space and time—these elementary needs and instincts, and then to study the conditions that may best satisfy them rationally.

This method, in a more or less confused form, is already to be found in the Utopian voyages, in the *History of the Sevarambes,* in the *Austral Land,* in the *Voyages of Jacques Massé,* in the *Isle of Calejava.* Denys Veiras, Tyssot de Patot, and the others describe various social groups that are supposed to have been already established somewhere, rationally, in order to satisfy the first and reasonable tendencies of human beings. That is fundamentally the method of Rousseau in his first *Discourse on the Sciences and the Arts.* Rousseau proposes above all, in analyzing the actual requirements of civilized man, to determine what is primitive and consequently legitimate (that is to say, family life and the common interests of the larger social group) and what is merely a complication and a perversion (intellectual curiosity, the arts, luxury). It is especially the method of Helvétius and d'Holbach. Neither Helvétius nor d'Holbach was a pure rationalist; and we shall discuss later what they required of observation and experience. But after all, Helvétius proposes to reconstruct the ideal society by the universal psychology of the human spirit. In *Discourse I* of Helvétius' *Of the Mind: Of the Mind in Itself,* we see that the mind is a plastic substance that is always the same everywhere and consequently able to assume any form. This brings us to *Discourse II. Of the Mind in Relation to Society,* in which it is shown that the mind in its individual manifestations is entirely influenced by social conditions; and to *Discourse III,* in which we see that by education we can fashion the type of man, hence the type of society, that we desire. D'Holbach, who has undoubtedly been schooled by Diderot, does not accept this rather naïve psychology of Helvétius. He knows that a mind at birth is subject to the powerful prenatal influences of race and heredity. But nevertheless he finds (particularly in his *Natural Politics or Discourses on the True Principles of Government,* 1773) certain primary needs, certain natural and consequently reasonable tendencies, the satisfaction of which can be rationally assured: the instinct of sociability, which is coexistent with the egotistic instinct; the spontaneous instinct of sacrifice, to which egotism consents for its own interest, inseparable as it is from the common interest. The art of legislating and of governing is the rationalized art of founding upon these first, permanent, universal needs the rights and duties of authority and of citizens, the methods of education, rewards and penalties, and so on.

The second method is no longer strictly abstract. In the eighteenth century men learned quickly enough to distrust Cartesian principles and universal reason. They realized that it is difficult to create a given form of society by adding together a certain number of identical minds, as the geometrician divides a hundred square feet into a hundred strictly identical parts. The starting point is therefore no longer the primitive mind, but primitive society. Thus one avoids an obscure hypothesis, that of the passage from individual egotism to the social spirit. But even so one proceeds from the outset by hypotheses, and the method is analogous to the psychological method. The psychological method tried to do away with all that was not primitive in the mind; the social method tries to rediscover what is primitive in the complexity of contemporary societies. It is a method that one might call "natural" in the sense that it purports to be founded on the study of that form of society that is constituted only according to the exigencies of nature.

The great master of this doctrine is undoubtedly J.-J. Rousseau, the Rousseau of the *Discourse on the Origin of Inequality among Men* (1754). Even he is not, or at least does not think he is, a theorist pure and simple. He desires—as we shall demonstrate—to support his hypotheses by facts. But Rousseau had very few facts available to reconstruct primitive society. He supplements therefore; he supposes. He finally arrives (or thinks he does) at social groups which are founded only on the basis of family life, on the natural inclination for mutual aid, and which know neither property nor the division of labor. Later, as soon as the earth is cultivated, there appear property, industry, commerce, and with them inequality, the vices of some, the misery and the envy of others, despotism, social evils. The *Letter to d'Alembert* is the application of the general thesis to a particular case, the misdeeds of the theater.

But if Rousseau gave this doctrine its splendor and its power, and if he revealed its profound consequences, it was by no means original with him; as a matter of fact, it was already quite old by 1754. For a long time missionaries and travelers had been visiting savages who lived, or who seemed to live, in a state of nature, in tents or in huts, without theaters, without books, without colleges, and without parliaments. At first their customs had been described; then from the sixteenth century (that becomes quite evident in reading Montaigne), particularly at the end of the seventeenth century, and throughout the eighteenth, these savages had been judged and compared with civilized men. Almost always the comparison with civilized society had resulted favorably for these savages as against the pretended wisdom of the so-called civilized peoples. And those who praised the simplicity and the good nature of the savage races were almost always missionaries and respectable people, who presumably would not be lying. Thus, in reasoning about society in a state of nature, neither Rousseau nor those who preceded or followed him discussed the matter in the abstract or from a purely hypothetical point of view. On the contrary, they based their studies on what they considered an assured reality. To believe in the happiness of a society reduced to the simplest conventions of social life was not merely to imagine another Utopia; it was to accept an observed fact.

However that may be, Rousseau and the others used and abused this information. In the seventeenth century there are about seventy works in which the savages are discussed or eulogized. There are at least sixty from about 1700 to 1750; and dramatic authors and romancers abundantly exploit the theme of Caribbean or Huron wisdom and felicity. Let us here recall the *Isle of Reason* of Marivaux, the Troglodytes of the *Persian Letters,* the savage Abaquis of the abbé Prévost's *Cleveland*, the *Adventures of M. Robert Chevalier, Called de Beauchêne* by Lesage, the *Alzire* of Voltaire, the *Peruvian Letters* of Mme de Graffigny. In this as in other matters, Rousseau sets the fashion. What was originally mere curiosity or diversion becomes through his influence bitter regret, an imperious sort of nostalgia. One no longer merely thinks of life in a state of nature; one vehemently aspires to it.

And there is almost literally not a single poet, novelist, "legislator," moralist, who does not write his idyl, his tale, his treatise, or his chapter on this topic. One might cite a hundred important works or texts in this connection. There are the poets, Saint-Lambert, Léonard, Parny; the authors of novels and tales, Voltaire, Marmontel, Restif de la Bretonne, Dorat, Bernardin de Saint-Pierre; the dramatic authors, Favart, Chamfort, and others. Political writers are almost all in agreement with Rousseau. Morelly (*Code of Nature*, 1755) studies "the condition of men on emerging from the state of nature" and "the admirable humanitarian traits of the peoples of America, who might well call us savages." Mably pleads for the savages of the United States as against the peoples who cultivate commerce and who cherish wealth. Raynal admires in turn the Paraguayans, the Indians, the Caribbeans, the Hottentots. Brissot de Warville praises the law of nature and Tahiti; Delisle de Sales is in agreement with Brissot. Linguet, who detests the philosophers, loves the savages as much as they do. The pamphleteers who multiply after 1770 become lyrical in speaking of the savages: "Oh, happy nations! Oh, lovable creatures! What gentleness of morals! What simplicity of law and custom!" (Rouillé d'Orfeuil, *The Alembic of the Laws,* 1773).

The consequences of the two methods.— The two methods, psychological and "natural," involved apparently quite different consequences. The analysis of the human mind evidently revealed a definite progress. Racine, Locke, and Newton were superior to the sorcerers of the savages, or even to the "philosophers" and the astronomers of the Parsees and the Egyptians. They were far superior, indeed, not through "enthusiasm" or "sentiment" but through reasoning powers. It is methodic and reasoning intelligence that has assured the progress of the human mind; why not believe then that this intelligence can also assure collective progress, social progress? Society then has a philosophical future before it, a future that may well be prepared by the philosophers and by those who will listen to them. Most of the philosophers have believed in this future, in their rôle, and in that of their disciples. They have written not for the rabble, which for a long time will be incapable of understanding them, but for those who can influence the instruction of the rabble, who can give it laws and form its morals. The entire hope of Voltaire, d'Alembert, Helvétius, and even Diderot is that a day will come "when philosophers will be kings, or at least kings philosophers." Social progress, therefore lies in a rational organization of society by philosophical intelligence.

This hope is divined in the *Preliminary Discourse* of the *Encyclopedia*, in which d'Alembert describes the progress of the human mind It is likewise manifest in the *Historical Sketch of the Human Mind* of Condorcet (1794). It would seem that all previous human efforts have been directed to the end of perfecting the reason of a Condorcet and his friends, and that their task in return is to assure the happiness of men.

The conclusion reached by the "natural" method is apparently quite different. In revealing the elementary forces of human society it does not judge that they are rudimentary. On the contrary it teaches, as often as not, that they are the best social forms and that the unhappiness of man is due to his not having been able to maintain them. Progress, therefore, lies not in the perfecting of society but in the renunciation of pretended perfection. It lies not in progress but in a return to a former status. And this return, far from dignifying the rôle of intelligence, will on the contrary suppress such mental activities as are useless or dangerous.

But Rousseau had nothing to do with this particular belief, whatever Voltaire (and many critics since his time) may say. He explained indeed that man was never happier than he was when he roamed the savannas with his little family group, possessing nothing but his bow and arrow or his club. But he said, and repeated on many occasions, that one cannot set back the hands of time and that society cannot be remade by mere philosophical demonstration. One may save society from the last fatal plunge into the abyss; but one cannot restore it to its original status. Whenever Rousseau writes from the practical point of view, for Geneva in the *Letter to d'Alembert* or the *Letters from the Mountain,* for the Corsicans in the *Letter to M. Buttafoco,* for the Poles in the *Considerations on the Government of Poland,* he is thinking of contemporary Genevans, Corsicans, Poles, not of "citizens of the world" or of neophytes of the state of nature. The *Social Contract* is another type of work and we shall discuss it later. But before Rousseau and after his time there were bolder dialecticians who did not hesitate to propose the abolition of the oldest forms of social life, such as property. The *History of the Sevarambes* and the *Telephus* of Pechméja (1784) evoke communism only as a romantic Utopia. The curate, Meslier, in his *Testament,* which had been circulating in manuscript since 1730, and the minister, d'Argenson, already speak of it more seriously. Morelly particularly, in his *Basiliade* (1753) and his *Code of Nature* (1775) proposes with due conviction that we return to a communistic state: "Fundamental and sacred laws: Nothing is to belong to any person except the objects that he will actually use for his needs or his pleasures or his daily toil." At the approach of the Revolution the makers of systems, some of whom obviously take delight in talking wildly, suggest or even definitely postulate socialistic systems. But on the whole, these are sporadic whims that find but few supporters; and indeed nothing before the Revolution indicates that they exercise any influence. Almost invariably, indeed, the two methods, far from following their diverging paths, have taken crossroads on which they very quickly meet.

Without ceasing to believe in the progress of the human mind and in the future of philosophic reason, the defenders of this progress are quite willing to admit that not everything is flawless in the apparent perfection of our civilized minds. There may be many "prejudices" among ideas that seem the most reasonable at first glance; and the "reason" of civilized men might find much to learn from "natural reason." The savages show us in a pure state, so to speak, precisely that universal good sense of which philosophical reason is but the perfected development. It is because of this that Voltaire, who does not like Rousseau's savages, may display so much indulgence for his own: "I fear that I cannot attain to the natural good sense of this almost savage child" [the Huron in the *Ingenuous Man*]. It is because of this that Diderot, who has not the slightest desire to renounce the arts or the sciences or even property, takes delight in giving us a scandalous and touching description of the happiness of the Tahitians. On the other hand the advocates of "natural" society generally do not deny that one cannot return to a pure state of nature; one can only find suggestions of that state in the course of one's studies. Only philosophical reason is capable of discerning these mere suggestions, of interpreting them, of deriving from them lessons applicable to the present time. Thus, partisans of both the psychological and the "natural" methods find a common meeting ground in "philosophy."

It is very true that this philosophy is an abstract rationalizing tendency that purports

to legislate absolutely. Tocqueville, Taine,
Cournot, and others have spoken of this fondness of the eighteenth century for speculation
in the field of abstract politics. They have ad-
duced all the instances that we have examined,
and others besides. They have recalled, aptly
enough, that almost all our philosophers,
whether they regret the state of nature or
whether they distrust it, take as their point of
departure a social contract or pact concluded
by reason in view of a reasonable social existence. This rational contract is in the *Social
Contract* of Rousseau; it is in Mably; it is in
d'Holbach (*Natural Politics. Discourse I, §6:
Of the Social Pact*). Now this pact is an argument; it is not a reality. And Tocqueville,
Taine, and Cournot were astonished or indignant at the fact that our philosophers thus
evolved "an abstract and literary type of politics," that they ignored the invincible realities
of social traditions, that by virtue of reasoning
beyond the bounds of time they led our national life, guided until then by time and quite
unable to live without it, into the most absurd
Utopias. "What a frightful spectacle!" It is
not for me to say whether all this was beneficial or fatal. But it is easy to prove that the
"frightful spectacle" never existed, save in the

imaginations of Tocqueville, Taine, and Cournot. It is true that the eighteenth century had a marked inclination for abstract reasoning; but it also displayed a new inclination (and all the more eager and profound because it was new) for the realities, for observation, and for experience.

Part III

THE NEW SPIRIT
OBSERVATION AND EXPERIENCE

CHAPTER I

THE CONSCIOUSNESS OF HUMAN DIVERSITY AND COMPLEXITY

Historical note.—Montesquieu (1689-1755) was a councilor, then president of the Parliament of Guyenne. He lived at first at Bordeaux or at Paris, frequenting the *salons,* interesting himself in science (he read papers on the *Causes of the Echo,* the *Use of the Renal Glands* and the *Weight of Bodies* before the Academy of Bordeaux). In 1721 he published the witty and trenchant *Persian Letters,* which brought him immediate celebrity. He left Bordeaux for Paris, published the *Dialogue of Sylla and Eucrates* (1722) and the gallant poem in prose of the *Temple of Cnidus* (1725) and was elected to the Academy. In 1726 he sold his president's commission, traveled (in 1728-1729) in Germany, Austria, Hungary, Italy, Switzerland, and Holland, examining, inquiring, taking notes; he resided in England from 1729 to 1731. On his return he established himself in his château of la Brède, where he published in 1734 the *Considerations on the Causes of the Greatness of the Romans and Their Decline* and in 1748 the *Spirit of the Laws,* which enjoyed tremendous popularity. Suffering, half-blind, he published thereafter only a few pamphlets.

The two chief writers of comic operas, highly renowned in the eighteenth century, were Favart (1710-1792), who produced the *Seeker of Wit* (1741), then, doubtless in collaboration with his wife, *Annette and Lubin* (1762), *The Reapers* (1764), etc.; and Sedaine (1717-1797), who wrote *Rose and Colas* (1764), *The Wooden Shoes* (1768), *The Deserter* (1769), etc. and a "drama," *The Unwitting Philosopher* (1765).

Geography and history.—The classical spirit is in part the feeling for unity and the constant effort to attain it. Racine, Boileau, and Descartes do not doubt that there are universal and permanent archetypes of beauty and of reason, and that the Phædra of Euripides and that of Racine and a Roxana of the Great Harem could understand each other perfectly. Without doubt certain reservations are made even in the classical period; there is a certain curiosity and uncertainty. But on the whole, classical philosophy and literature suppress time and space. The eighteenth century does much to rediscover them.

First of all, it is the century of travels. Voltaire visits England, Germany, Switzerland, and Holland. Montesquieu travels for three years in Germany, Switzerland, Italy, and England. Rousseau travels more or less unwillingly in Italy, Germany, and England. Diderot visits Holland, Germany, and Russia. Beaumarchais carries on his intrigues throughout Europe, from Spain to England or Austria. D'Holbach knows Germany and England well. Condillac is the tutor of the Prince of Parma. Bernardin de Saint-Pierre is a restless wanderer, driven by his uneasy temperament to never-ending travels throughout all Europe. Chénier knows England well, and visits Italy. For those who do not travel or who cannot travel widely enough, there exists a huge literature of well-documented and picturesque accounts of voyages. There is the collection, continued for more than seventy years, of the *Edifying and Curious Letters Written from Foreign Missions*. There is the abbé Prévost's *General History of Voyages*, in twenty-one volumes, published during a period of twenty-five years; this *History* brought him more readers and wealth than his novels. There are luxurious publications, folio volumes, adorned with numerous engravings: *Picturesque Travels in Greece* by Choiseul-Gouffier, *Topographical and Picturesque Sketches of Switzerland* by J.-B. Delaborde and Zurlauben, *Picturesque Travels in Naples and Sicily* by the abbé de Saint-Non, and a hundred other tales, memoirs, and diaries, which lead the reader over continents and oceans. This is also the period of a new series of great maritime voyages of discovery; pub-

lic opinion is passionately interested. Readers
eagerly devour the *Voyage Around the World*
by Admiral Anson and the account of the explorations of Cook and Bougainville.

The great writers of the century reflect this
taste for world-wide travel in both their serious and their lighter works. Novels, tales,
tragedies, dramas, comedies, and comic operas
often have Oriental, Chinese, Egyptian, Peruvian, and Indian personages. Without doubt,
the exoticism of these productions very often
consists of a costume or a disguise. Babylon
is Paris and the "dervishes" are French
priests. But then too the exoticism is often sincere: the author makes an effort to be neither
Parisian, nor French, nor European, nor civilized. Instead of the universal man who is of
every country, he wishes to portray the man
who is emphatically not of our country; he
asks the reader to consider the diversity of customs, the infinite variety of usages and beliefs. The Persians of the *Persian Letters* of
Montesquieu have genuinely Persian ideas
concerning marriage and the relations between the two sexes. Voltaire really desires to
be "Chinese" in the *Orphan of China* and
"American" in *Alzire*, just as Mme de Graffigny is, or endeavors to be, "Peruvian" in the

Peruvian Letters, Marmontel an "Inca" in the *Incas*; and other authors desire to be in turn "Hurons," "Algonquins," or "Tahitians." Chénier proposes to write his *America*. The descriptive poems of Roucher and Saint-Lambert conjure up deserts, virgin forests, the tropics. The *Voyage to Mauritius* and the *Studies of Nature* of Bernardin de Saint-Pierre are most surprising studies that take us from the frozen steppes to the radiant shores of Mauritius. The *Natural History* of Buffon represents a voyage to every clime. It is true, indeed, that there is perhaps a permanent and universal principle in man. But men are coming to agree that there is an animal part in man that changes, and they are beginning to believe that it influences the spiritual part.

Moreover, history serves to confirm the teachings of geography. As we have observed, the historical sense was very slow in developing and it remained hesitant, and often naïve, to the very end. However, men were not slow in acquiring a feeling for the diversity of different epochs. From this viewpoint Voltaire really created or, rather, completed the creation of modern history. His *Essay on the Customs and the Essential Spirit of Nations* is a judicious and penetrating study of the differ-ence of customs and of the national spirit in all races and periods. Of course there are defects in his treatment. He is unable to discern whatever runs counter to his prejudices as a philosopher and a polemic. He is unaware of mystic forces. He does not understand that nations and races may be formed, maintained, and upheld by beliefs which are apparently irrational but which nevertheless are in fact beneficial forces. Consequently, he makes many foolish statements about the Middle Ages, about the Orient, about anything that thwarts his habits of analysis and "good sense." But however that may be, he wrote his *Essay* in order to demonstrate that human customs are infinitely variegated, and that there is no one essential "spirit" that is common to all nations.

In an even clearer fashion than the *Essay on Customs,* the *Spirit of the Laws* of Montesquieu imposed the idea that in order to understand the history and the institutions of men, it was necessary to emphasize not their resemblances but their differences. Without doubt, the *Spirit of the Laws* is in part deduced by that argumentative type of reasoning that attempts to draw from the diversity of human laws the unity and simplicity of rational laws.

Montesquieu does not study despotisms, monarchies, republics, but rather *Despotism, Monarchy,* the *Republic*; and he is convinced, or seems to be convinced, that from Pekin to London, from the Esquimaux to the Patagonians, these governmental forms are based on the principles that are postulated by the reason of Montesquieu. Again, there is in the *Spirit of the Laws* an ideal of the organization of the laws that has all the appearance of a rational ideal. The fine "balance of power," based upon a combination of acting forces and of stabilizing forces, is indeed constructed like an abstract theory of the perfect government. Yet, behind the theory there exists (and no reader is unaware of the fact) the precise and living reality of England. To serve as a basis for the study of the despotic, monarchical, and republican principles, there is the historical and realistic study of despotisms, monarchies, republics. There is the demonstration that humanity has not the unfettered power to choose rationally its principles of government. It is governed by climate and race. It must be remembered that Montesquieu's theories about government and the "balance of power" do not represent the essential part of his work. Nor do they constitute the most influential part:

108 EIGHTEENTH CENTURY FRENCH THOUGHT

for the "wise harmony" of the English constitution was very soon and very vehemently dis-
puted. What proved most fascinating to his
readers, and what Montesquieu himself preferred, without doubt, was the study not of the
harmonizing elements but of the diversifying
elements of the laws.

We find this study in those books of the
Spirit of the Laws in which Montesquieu considers in turn how the laws must be adapted to
the climate, to the "habitat," to the "general
spirit." In a word, it is the realistic theory
that Montesquieu opposes to the rational theories of a Grotius or of a Puffendorf. He no
longer seeks the law that is most conformable
theoretically to the nature or to the reason of
man. Laws "are the necessary relationships
which are derived from the nature of things."
That is to say that there are as many relationships as there are "things." These "things"
are: hot or cold climate, fertile or sterile soil,
mountainous or level country, maritime or in-
land position, finally the "general spirit," that
is, the customs gradually evolved by the generations subjected to this climate and to this
habitat. These customs are necessarily very diverse, depending upon their localization in
China, France, Holland, or Italy. The laws

that will prove beneficial for varying communities will be those that are founded upon these differences and not upon the common element that one may discover, by the process of reasoning, in Chinese, Frenchmen, Dutchmen, or Italians. Half of the *Spirit of the Laws* is a geographical study (if one may call it that) of the laws. It does not represent mere theorizing, but realistic observation.

As a protest against the abstract systems and the theoretical and fatal rationalism of the philosophers of the eighteenth century, Taine presented the realities that fashion human souls: the environment, the race, and the critical moment of history. But it was precisely in the eighteenth century that the theory of environment and race was organized by Montesquieu and many others. Taine realized, indeed, that he had not invented it; but he thought that before his time it had been only a fleeting idea that appealed to but few men. On the contrary, in the eighteenth century this idea was commonly held, discussed at great length, and constantly perfected. It influences literature, politics, and philosophy. The theory of climate is already outlined in the learned Baillet, in Fénelon, Chardin, La Motte-Houdart, Huet, Fontenelle, the abbé Dubos, at the end

of the seventeenth century and in the first third
of the eighteenth. It soon becomes more precise in Voltaire (in spite of certain reserves),
d'Argens, Turgot, Diderot. And it is developed still further toward 1760 by discussions
and dissertations in which it often seems that
it is Taine himself who is reasoning. "The element that produces great works," says Diderot,
"is . . . the fortunate influence of customs,
usages, and climate." As Turgot explains it,
Ossian is merely the climate of Caledonia.
"The man of genius," as Helvétius demonstrates, "is only the product of the circumstances in which he happens to find himself";
thus is explained the neglect that had befallen
Corneille after that period of perfervid admiration when his personages were "analogous
to the spirit of the century." The *Library of
Novels* proposes to publish "a small literary
geography." In 1765 the abbé Pichon publishes the *Physics of History*; and in 1769 J.-
L. Castilhon writes his *Considerations on the
Physical and Moral Causes of Diversity in
the Genius, Customs, and Government of Nations*.

Literature.—If climate and race act upon
the customs and laws of nations, they also act
upon literature; and literature can make the

differences in climate and race apparent to those who do not travel in Italy, in England, or in the Orient; that is to say, to the great majority of men. All manner of foreign books now come to them in translation. In the eighteenth century, and especially in the second half of the century, literature becomes genuinely "cosmopolitan": that statement is often made, either in pride or regret. Without doubt, foreign works had always enjoyed a certain vogue in France: our sixteenth century was schooled in large part by Italy and to a lesser degree by Spain, our seventeenth century by Spain and, to a lesser degree, by Italy, the eighteenth century by Italy and practically not at all by Spain. But in the sixteenth and seventeenth centuries Italians and Spaniards were read because they resembled Frenchmen. Never did one say: "We read foreign works because they are foreign and so that we may temporarily forget our own land." On the contrary, in the eighteenth century curiosity leads men to the study of the most diverse peoples for the sheer pleasure in diversity. La Fontaine said that he read authors "from the North and from the South": but for him "North" was only a figure of speech and did not extend beyond the Seine. In the eighteenth century, however, "North" represents England, Germany, Scandinavia, and indeed every people that has a literature. Cosmopolitan taste becomes a mania. It is "Anglomania" and "foreign mania." The movement suddenly becomes powerful. After 1750 it is irresistible.

To indicate its extent it would be necessary to enumerate all the translations or adaptations of works of every land: English, Swiss, German, Persian, Hindu, Dutch, Danish. The list would be interminable. Let us only note that from 1750 to the Revolution more than a hundred English novels are translated or adapted. I have counted the novels included in the catalogue of five hundred private libraries from 1740 to 1760. The items that are most frequently found (second only to the *Peruvian Letters* of Mme de Graffigny) are novels by Richardson and Fielding. Of the nine novels that are catalogued most frequently in these libraries, one finds 1698 volumes of English novels as against 497 volumes of French novels. The *Bibliographical Manual of French Literature* by Lanson, which is a manual and which necessarily restricts itself to the essentials, enumerates 20 translations from the Spanish, 52 from the Italian, 245 from the English, 76 from the German, 20 from various other literatures. The *Foreign Journal* is founded in order to disseminate knowledge about foreign literatures. But even journals like the *Literary Yearbook* of Fréron, the *Literary Gazette* of Arnaud and Suard, and the *Encyclopedic Journal* devote much space to analyses of works which are not French.

Evidently, in the course of the ninety years from 1700 to the Revolution, there is evolution, discussion, reaction. Certain foreigners do not count, or hardly count at all, because they are only apparently foreigners or because the translations easily eliminate whatever is not in strict accordance with French taste. It is true, nevertheless, that, while it remains French, the prevalent literary taste becomes, at first gradually, then boldly, a different sort of taste and even a more or less direct negation of classical taste, classical rules, classical reason. There is no romantic literary school toward 1770 or 1780, for the simple reason that the rebels have not formed a definite group, and likewise because they produce only mediocre works to justify their audacious theories. But whatever the Romantic School will scorn in the nineteenth century has already been condemned and reviled in the eighteenth and almost everything that the Romanticists will believe that they have originated has already been discovered.

In spite of certain reserves, the classical principle is that there exists an immutable model of beauty. There has always been a good or a bad taste that remains eternally the same; and the precise rules of this taste may be very exactly revealed. In this matter the *Quarrel between the Ancients and the Moderns* brings into opposition not diverse doctrines but diverse interpretations of the Doctrine. Boileau, Racine, La Bruyère, and the others maintain that the ancients discovered these rules and applied them with such perfection that modern writers should imitate them, and at most can only succeed in equaling them. Perrault, La Motte, and Fontenelle think, on the contrary, that the science of the Beautiful, like all sciences, should progress with time and experience, and that the moderns are capable of writing better tragedies or epics, just as they actually have produced better work in mathematics and astronomy. But the object of their researches remains the same: it is absolute beauty. Perrault says that

> The wondrous ideas of the immutably fair
> Are carefully kept in a palace rare.

CONSCIOUSNESS OF HUMAN DIVERSITY   115

However, toward 1730 men begin to believe
that this palace will never be discovered because it does not exist. They perceive that all
those who claim to have penetrated therein
have given radically different descriptions of
it. And yet there might be at least some sem-
blance of harmony if one read only Sophocles,
Vergil, Horace, Racine, the Greeks, the Lat-
ins, the writers of the seventeenth century. But
one discovers the *Arabian Nights*, Milton,
Swift, Shakespeare, Dante. Even if they are
called barbarians, it must be admitted that
they are admired by the English and the
Italians. Does that not indicate that the Beautiful is "relative" and that there is no "absolute"
taste? Before 1750 men hesitate to adopt this
skeptical doctrine. They prop up, on one side,
the ideal of permanent beauty that they under-
mine on the other. But nevertheless skepticism
is about to impose itself. The abbé Dubos, in a
celebrated book that becomes a classic in a few
years (*Reflections on Poetry and Painting*,
1719), adopts certain viewpoints that confirm
those of Boileau: it is true that the great
Greek, Latin, French writers have indeed discovered the Beautiful, which is perfect and
unique. But it is bootless to attempt to analyze
it and to teach it by means of reason. One

"feels" it, and there is no other proof of this feeling than its existence and its permanence. Toward 1750 the theorists are not in exact agreement as to precisely how much one should grant to feeling and how much to reason. But by that time it is a general, commonplace, and even academic doctrine that it is impossible to believe in a permanent ideal of beauty, in methodical and universal rules of taste. Diderot writes for the *Encyclopedia* an article on the *Beautiful* which is added to the specimen *Prospectus* and which consequently was not chosen to scandalize prospective subscribers. In this article Diderot condemns the æsthetic ideas of the Boileaus and the Perraults, even though he does not mention their names; he demonstrates the impossibility of the ideal of Universal Beauty; he concludes that there are sundry reasons why men differ in their conception of the Beautiful. This does not merely represent the boldness of Diderot's peculiar philosophy or romanticism. When one studies the article carefully, one perceives that for the most part it is merely an intelligent compilation of the theories of those whom Diderot names in certain cases: Father André, Hutcheson, Shaftesbury, Father Buffier, and others. Many of these authorities are or

have been educators; what they say is actually
being taught. It is decidedly no longer believed that the Beautiful may be demonstrated
and determined by reason alone.

It is true that it is a far cry from a philosophy of the Beautiful to actual literary practice. But that chasm is soon bridged. After
1760, and in even greater profusion after 1770,
there are dozens of treatises and chapters, and
hundreds of remarks and notes, in which the
precepts so dear to Boileau are rejected.

Even the most venerated rules are crumbling. Very often the dramas of Diderot, of
L.-S. Mercier, of Baculard d'Arnaud, and
others respect the rule of the three unities.
Very often, too, they ignore it and even deride
it; and with it the flimsy edifice of literary
rules crashes to the ground. "Genius that is
enlightened by profound sagacity judges
usage before submitting to it. . . . Rules, precepts, customs, nothing can impede it; nothing can slacken the rapidity of its course; from
its very first soaring, it wings its way to the
sublime." This genius is like "a cliff, the
height and the steepness of which terrify us;
its crest, towering up, seems to be suspended
aloft." It is Séran de la Tour who speaks thus
in 1762. He is still quite polite about the

matter. Others like L.-S. Mercier (1778) or
Dorat-Cubières (1787) are more insolent.
"What do I care about these worthless Rules?
. . . Do you think I need them to guide me in
my poetic transports?" "At last the flag of
literary warfare is floating in the breeze. . . .
Richardson moves me far more than all the
tragedies of the divine Racine. . . . This is all
blasphemy, without doubt." But Racine "has
killed art."

In order to resuscitate art, it is decided to
ignore the injunctions to "respect the spectators" and to "speak to the soul and not to the
body." French actors announce, without in the
least intending to be humorous, that they have
spirituous liquors available for any ladies in
the audience who may faint during a performance. And to provoke these fainting
spells they vie in lavishing scaffolds, chambers with black hangings, coffins, death's-
heads, ghosts, all the bric-à-brac that will be so
prominently displayed twenty years later by
Pixérécourt and the "boulevard of crime."

Even style and versification are gliding
down the slope that leads from rules to liberty, from "reason" to the "rights of genius." J.-
J. Rousseau scoffs at the "noble" style and at
those blockheads of Frenchmen who are un-

willing to use the word "blockhead." But at
the very time that he is scoffing, the purists,
despite stubborn resistance, are already beginning to give ground. Even the authors of
the "great poems," of those "descriptive
poems" that take the place of the epic, claim
the right to treat any subject, even in verse,
with words of everyday usage. And such poets
include not only Chénier and Saint-Lambert,
who are philosophers, or Roucher, who is a
"sentimental soul," but men like Delille, who
is an abbé and an educator, who is the glory
of the University and whose boldness inaugu-
rates the fashion of poetry devoted to salads,
to watercress, to plows, to the dung-pile, to
cattle, to

> . . . the fertile cow
> Which can now freely enter your parks or my verse.

The cæsura of the Alexandrine line follows
the fate of restricted vocabulary and circum-
locutions. The versification of Chénier, which
will delight the Romantics, is no bolder than
that of Roucher, of the Fontanes of the old
régime, even of Delille. In certain respects he
is not as bold as they: he is less addicted to
ternary divisions and overlapping lines. Liberty in versification was demanded and even

attempted fifty years before Hugo's *Autumn Leaves*, the versification of which is not much more audacious than that of Roucher and Fontanes.

Finally—and this is a symbol of the new era in literature—it is the venerated chieftain of classical reason who is discussed, refuted, and even reviled. On occasion Boileau is treated more unceremoniously than he had ever treated Saint-Amand or Scudéry. To be sure, he has some illustrious defenders. In 1785 the Academy assigns his eulogy as the topic for a literary competition; and Daunou, who wins the prize, does not spare his compliments. But the academicians themselves, and the most academic of the writers, have certain scruples in the matter and defend Boileau in half-hearted fashion. Voltaire, Marmontel, La Harpe, and others maintain that he was a great man and that his lessons are still valid. But when they are no longer enraged by the insolence of his antagonists, and when they consider the matter dispassionately, they admit that Boileau was too cold and too calculating to be a great man. Others insist that he was essentially stupid, and they vigorously assail him. "He has no enthusiasm, no energy, no warmth." "Every young man who feels

that he has a certain creative talent should
first of all throw into the fire all the treatises
on poetic art, beginning with that of Boileau."
That is the opinion of Mercier and of Cu-
bières, but it is shared by many others. At Neuchâtel, in Switzerland, "even the most insignificant pygmy of our literature thinks himself
greatly superior to Boileau." The rational
ideal of the Beautiful, and the poetic sublima-
tion of reason, are about to crumble into the
dust.

CHAPTER II

THE EXPERIMENTAL
SCIENCES

Historical note.—Buffon (1707-1788) was born in the château of Montbard, Burgundy. After a rather adventurous youth, he acquired a deep interest in the study of physics and natural history. In 1739 he became the superintendent of the king's zoölogical garden. The first three volumes of his *Natural History* appeared in 1749 (*Theory of the Earth and General Views on Generation and on Man*). Then he published in succession the *Quadrupeds* (1753-1767), the *Birds* (1770-1783), and the *Minerals* (1783-1788). *Supplements* appeared from 1774 to 1779 (among them the *Epochs of Nature,* 1778). Buffon had several collaborators: Daubenton for the anatomical descriptions, Guéneau de Montbéliard and the abbé Bexon for ornithology, Guyton de Morveau and Faujas de Saint-Fond for mineralogy.

Among the principal scientists or popularizers of science in the eighteenth century, special mention must be made of Réaumur (*Observations on the History of Insects,* 1734-1742, 6 vol.) and the abbé Nollet (*Lessons of Experimental Physics,* 1743, 8th edition, 1775; *The Art of Experimentation, or Advice to Amateur Physicists on the Choice, Construction, and Use of Apparatus,* etc., 1770).

The adversaries of experimental science.— Natural history and physics had been discussed long before the eighteenth century. Without going back as far as Pliny, bestiaries were abundant in the literatures of the Middle Ages; they compiled most indefatigably prodigies and marvels, tales of sirens, of seven-headed hydras, and of talking dragons. It would be a mistaken notion to believe that the authors and readers of the eighteenth century were much less naïve in their credulity. They believed in talking dogs, in the basilisk whose glance kills as surely as a pistol shot, in the Bohemian fountain that stays its flow when an impure woman has touched its waters, and in a hundred other manifestations of the devil's wiles or of the bounties of Providence. Above all, there is a general conviction that natural phenomena have been so contrived by Providence as to become the record of its power and its goodness. In the second half of the century there is hardly any belief in the basilisk or in the modesty of fountains. But natural history persists in remaining a mere chapter of theology. A good number of the geologists who precede Buffon, those whose history of the earth he discusses, are theologians by profession. One of the greatest books of the first half of the century—it will prove useful to Chateaubriand—is the *Existence of God Demon-*

strated by the Marvels of Nature, by Nieuwen-
tyt (1725). Another celebrated work is the
Spectacle of Nature by Pluche, consisting of
object lessons, the supreme lesson being the
exposition of the wisdom of God, who diver-
sified the green coloring of plants in order to
rest our eyes and who created tides so that vessels might be enabled to enter their harbors.
When Bernardin de Saint-Pierre is moved by
the goodness of Providence, which gave ribs
to the melon so that it might more readily be
eaten in a family group, he was merely following one of the most commonplace traditions of the century. One might enumerate at
great length the physicists and the naturalists
who avail themselves of animals, plants, peb-
bles, and stars in order to explain and justify
Genesis, the Bible, the miracles, the deluge
and Noah's ark, and, if need be, to refute Galileo, Copernicus, and Newton.

A hundred or a hundred and fifty years before, there existed a surer method of refuting
Galileo, which was to bid him hold his peace.
But the insolence of Galileo might well be renewed, and impious physicists might give explanations of the history of the world and the
mystery of things that would not be in agreement with Genesis and the theologians. That

is what happened in the case of a certain de Maillet in his *Telliamed* (1748). But de Maillet combined so much fanciful nonsense with his ingenious ideas that he ran no risk of becoming an authority. So obscure a book was merely condemned without much ado. But matters were not so simple in M. de Buffon's case. "In his *History of the Earth*," says d'Argenson, "he really contradicts Genesis in every particular." If he does not contradict it explicitly, it is difficult to see how his explanations can be made to harmonize with the sacred texts. Now M. de Buffon was famous from the very outset: the *Natural History* was vaunted as an immortal work. Science, instead of being the handmaid of a majestic theology, was now brazenly contradicting it, or at least declaring itself independent of it. The theologians were becoming uneasy: "The devout," said d'Argenson, "are furious." The Sorbonne, passing from mere opinion to action, condemned fourteen propositions found in the *Natural History* (1751). This was no mere Platonic condemnation. The consequence, after a brief respite, might be the condemnation of the book, or its destruction, or even the arrest of Buffon. Buffon detested "theological wrangling"; he proposed to the doctors of the

Sorbonne certain formulas of submission in which he abandoned "whatever might be contrary to the narration of Moses." The formulas were accepted, published at the beginning of the fourth volume, and the first three volumes continued to be freely sold.

But the dispute did not result in the triumph of Moses or of the theologians. The *History of the Earth* continued to present its facts and its observations without caring whether or not they were confirmed by Genesis. Public opinion began to believe that the decisions of a council of theologians might not suffice to refute observations and facts. Some other weapon must be sought.

The most orthodox and the most uncertain method was to demonstrate that Moses had anticipated all the geologists and that science merely confirmed revelation. "All the most certain and most undeniably established discoveries," said the naturalist, Bourguet, "contribute admirably to confirm the factual truths upon which religion is founded." This meant that science was useless or that it was, as in the past, the handmaid of theology. But henceforth curiosity and scientific bent were too strong for such an explanation as this. Other expedients were sought. The first was to grant the human mind full liberty in scientific research; religious scruples, theology, intervened only afterward. Thus scientific curiosity remains free provisionally; religion is only an ultimate source of control. "I proposed at the outset," says the Genevan, Deluc, "to consider only as a materialist the phenomena offered by the surface of our globe, putting entirely aside for the moment the relationship that they might bear to religion in the matter of the universal deluge. . . . I have employed the means of free research: principles, facts, consequences; and I have never consulted authority. Now that I have said all that I had to say on the subject . . . , let us consider the relation between Nature and Revelation." There was only one difficulty: that Nature might not agree at all with Revelation; and disagreements arose at the very first examination. For example, there was not a single naturalist who could believe that the world had been created in six days. The difficulty was avoided by the method of *interpretation*. Divine wisdom had necessarily expressed itself in human language, in words the sense of which could not be rigorously determined. Scientists could therefore seek in the vague terminology of the Bible some precise meaning that would be in accordance with their discoveries. Besides, this wisdom had expressed itself briefly. It had revealed only the general outlines; it had relegated to human curiosity the task of establishing the details. This method of interpretation soon proved to be very successful. It is the method of Buffon, who demonstrates, in the preliminary explanations of his *Epochs of Nature*, that the *days* of Genesis can only signify *periods* or *epochs*. It was already the method of Pluche; on occasion, that of the very pious Needham, that of the not less pious Bonnet; and that which was ostensibly employed by the *Encyclopedia*, Boulanger, d'Holbach. "If your arguments drawn from the very nature of things are strong and conclusive, you may depart from literal interpretation in the explanation of the history of creation by Moses, and you may even do so without exposing yourself to adverse criticism." "One cannot doubt the reality of the deluge . . . , but it appears that, without abandoning the respect due to the evidence of Holy Scripture, it is legitimate for the naturalist to consider whether the deluge was really the cause of the phenomena we are about to consider."

This method, convenient as it was, was evidently very dangerous. It did not disturb Protestants like Deluc or Bonnet, familiar as they were with free examination; it was more menacing in the case of Catholic orthodoxy, which was attached to the principle of authority. The Sorbonne deliberated whether or not it should condemn the *Epochs* of Buffon in spite of his explanations; it was prevented from doing so only by fear of ridicule. And the broadest interpretation might not succeed in reconciling Moses and the facts. Consequently another solution was offered, the most satisfying of all, the most successful; a solution that will, doubtless, always be more or less successful. It is to the effect that there are truths of various sorts which are not to be supplemented or controlled, which develop on parallel planes, forever separated: the truths of faith or of the heart, and the truths of reason or of science; the truths requisite for the conduct of life—"pragmatic truths"—and those of constructive intelligence which explain the world. We can, then, be Christians on one hand, and scientists on the other; we can believe simultaneously in our holy books or dogmas, and in our observations and our experiments, even if they are mutually contradictory. That is the conviction or the affirma-

tion of almost everybody after 1750—that of
Needham, the abbé Nollet, Réaumur, Diderot
and others. Scientists generally have a sort of
dual rôle, that of Catholics and that of physicists. "In our capacity as Catholics," they say,
"we respect the authority of the holy books,
and we submit without analysis to whatever
faith proposes; but as physicists we believe
ourselves entitled to venture our conjectures.
And however contrary they may be to the
sacred texts, they nevertheless appear to us to
be probable."

A convenient solution, indeed, and one that
had another merit: it might be, and it often
was, sincere. Not, to be sure, with Diderot, but
with certain great scientists: Nollet, Needham, Réaumur and even Buffon. It was decisive and it was soothing. Thus science had
fought its last battle against theology, or
rather, against the despotism of ancient theology. It had freed itself.

The organization of experimental science.
—But it had gained the victory only because it
had deserved it. Before conquering others, it
had conquered itself, that is, it had rejected the
old idols and it had subjected itself to a rigid
discipline.

It purported to be an effort to understand

and to explain the world. Now this attempt was by no means the first. Scholastic philosophy was actually giving this explanation daily with the utmost assurance. But "assurance" in the matter was precisely what was no longer desired. With a certain amount of argumentation, supposedly logical, without any observation whatsoever, scholastic philosophy gave a comprehensive account of the visible and the invisible. It had done nothing but assemble words in which the men of the eighteenth century no longer found anything but a buzzing of syllables: "To know whether fecund matter, or the sensitive element, is to be found in a mixed act. Whether the specific unity of a science is based upon the unity of the motive by virtue of which we consent to its conclusions": such problems as these appeared to be no longer scientific problems but mere nonsense. Scholastic philosophy had been attacked as early as the close of the seventeenth century; the attacks were multiplied throughout the eighteenth. They gathered in one camp not only all the philosophers but also very pious people like the abbé Pluche, Trembley, the abbé Fromageot, President Rolland, and many others: "A puerile scaffolding . . . , a monstrous chaos . . . , a refuge of error and of bad faith." In the second half of the century, scholastic philosophy succumbs to the onslaughts of ridicule. It disappears almost completely, not indeed from philosophy, but from the scientific teaching of the colleges.

But there was another type of scholasticism to be overcome: it was the construction of theoretical systems. The human mind, not resigning itself to ignorance, elaborates sundry logical systems of the world and of universal truth. For a long time these systems had constituted all of science. "Two things are necessary in the study of physics," writes the educator, Denyse, in 1719, "experimentation and argumentation. We are going to begin with argumentation." It is the method followed by a great number of physicists who even spare themselves the trouble of argumentation. One finds in abundance works like the following: *Remarks on the Physical Principle of the Regeneration of Beings, of Movement, of Gravity and of Attraction; Philosophical Discourse on the Three Principles: Animal, Vegetable and Mineral; Dissertations on the Universal Electric Mechanism of Nature with Respect to Physics, Metaphysics, Politics, and Morals*. But these and other ridiculous systems are rapidly discredited. "I have heard," writes Condillac, "that one of these physicists, who congratulated himself on having a principle that would account for all the phenomena of chemistry, was so daring as to communicate his ideas to a skilled chemist. The latter, having been obliging enough to listen to the physicist, told him that there was only one difficulty: that the facts were not at all what he supposed them to be. 'Very well, then,' rejoined our physicist, 'just tell me what the facts are, so that I may explain them.'" Physicists of this category had been derided long before Condillac.

The philosophers, and many who are not philosophers, are united in heaping ridicule upon the universal systems which substitute for facts and experimentation the chimeras of their theoretical creations. "Let us not establish systems." "There has been too marked a tendency to construct systems." "Sensible people scorn what is known as systematic physics." The delight in generalization is a "mania" and its victims are "systematizers." That is the opinion of a hundred philosophers, physicists, naturalists, journalists, college teachers, Father Bougeant, Mairan, Nollet, Deluc, Bertrand, Condorcet, and others. And the *Treatise on Systems* by Condillac is a treatise against systems.

A famous episode took place in the course of this scientific warfare. We like to think of Buffon as a scrupulous man of science. Now it so happened that certain scientists of the eighteenth century, after critically examining Buffon's works, came to the apparently strange conclusion that he was an adventurer in science, a mere "systematizer," whose example was dangerous. His *Natural History* began with general explanations, with universal systems: it contained a *History of the Earth* which purported to give a full explanation of the formation of the earth, theories on generation and animal mechanism, that undertook to enlighten us concerning all the mysteries of life. Then too Buffon attacked the naturalists who, like Linnæus, contented themselves with describing and classifying, the "nomenclators." He proclaimed his liking for "broad views" and "general views." Contemporary scientists answered him almost unanimously, and in certain cases not very ceremoniously, that there was only one drawback: that was that these "broad views" were mere figments of the imagination. "I shall hardly belie public sentiment," writes the abbé Nonnotte in 1772, "when I say that M. de Buffon had merely the intention of composing a novel when he wrote his history of the formation of the earth." That is, indeed, the opinion of many illustrious critics and of others who are obscure: for instance, Grimm, Diderot, d'Alembert, Rouelle, Bonnet. Réaumur persuaded the abbé de Lignac to publish in 1751 and 1756 certain *Letters to an American* which are a violent criticism of Buffon; and the *Treatise on Animals* by Condillac is a treatise against the animal theories of Buffon.

In opposition to these "general systems," there were established at an early period the principles and the methods of experimental science. There was some knowledge of Bacon in France from the end of the seventeenth century, and a more detailed knowledge in the first half of the eighteenth. But his philosophy of experimental science was hardly popularized before 1750. Before that date the rôle played by facts, experimentation, and hypotheses had already been determined in really scientific circles. Buffon in an *Introduction* to a translation of the *Statics of Plants* by the Englishman, Hales (1735), Deslandes adapting a discourse of Musschenbroek in his treatise *On*

the Best Means of Conducting Experiments
(1735) had proposed rules that were almost
as rigorous as the classic rules of Stuart Mill:
"I may even say that in physics one should
seek experimentation as much as one should
fear systems. . . . It is by precise, rational,
and consistent experimentation that one forces
nature to reveal its secrets; all other methods
have never succeeded." And Deslandes, like
Buffon, determines very exactly what precise,
rational, and consistent experiments are. To-
wards 1750 one may say that these Baconian
and Newtonian ideas have become commonplace. In 1749 there is published a translation
of a *Grammar of the Philosophical Sciences,
or an Abridged Analysis of Modern Philosophy Based upon Experimentation* by the
Englishman, Martin; this is a sort of scholastic manual with questions and answers, and
at the same time an almost modern manual of
the experimental method.

This theory is put into practice by various
famous men. Even if Buffon does venture to
give his "broad views," he at least attempts to
justify them by precise facts, by minute observations, by patient experiments—for example, that on the cooling of masses of iron.
He is an indefatigable worker and the eight-

eenth century knows that he is. Moreover two other books on natural history are almost as celebrated as his own. These are the *Remarks on the Study of the History of Insects,* by Réaumur (1734-1742), and the *Remarks on a Certain Genus of Fresh-water Polyp with Horn-shaped Arms,* by Trembley (1744). Both are collections of attentive and rigorous observations and experiments. In the field of experimental physics Dagoumer was already making certain very popular experiments in 1701. But the abbé Nollet was the popularizer *par excellence* and he soon became famous. In 1734 he begins a course from which he banishes "all jargon and all speculation," in which his arguments consist of levers, lenses, furnaces, pneumatic machines. His listeners include persons "of every age, of both sexes, of all social strata." He is commissioned to give lessons to the duc de Chartres and to the Dauphin. Finally in 1753 there is created for him in the University of Paris a professorial chair of experimental physics and he thenceforth conducts what a contemporary calls "a school of philosophical taste."

There was, however, one temptation that this experimental philosophy found difficulty in resisting: it was to believe that in discovering the laws of nature, scientists were throwing light upon the infinite goodness of Providence. There were but few mechanists to affirm, as did Diderot, that the concatenation of causes and effects is indifferently beneficial or harmful to human interests. If Bernardin de Saint-Pierre could be extravagant with the prodigious candor of his optimism, it was because his contemporaries shared his viewpoint. Everything is created for man: that is the theme of many a work and chapter. Whales are dangerous for vessels, but the shark is the enemy of the whale; "consequently all animals were created for man, although we may not know the peculiar property and use of each." Even those who, like Diderot, Condillac, and Bertrand, are materialists or genuine scientists cannot resist the pleasure of believing that if nature left to itself is indifferent to the happiness of men, physics and natural history are solely intended to oblige nature to serve our interests. They would like to accept the explanation of Leclerc (1763), that the scientist "will study nature only in order that he may use it." Experimental philosophy did not desire to divorce itself from "economic," "humanitarian," or social philosophy.

The diffusion and the influence of science.
—The experimental sciences might have been
able to defend themselves and to organize
themselves without interesting the general
public, in a circle of scientists, theologians,
and some philosophers. But the sciences
aroused as much curiosity as did philosophy
in the eighteenth century; and they doubtless
had more devotees.

The philosophers themselves cultivated the
sciences assiduously, as much so, indeed, as
they cultivated Descartes, Spinoza, or Locke.
Voltaire is rather especially devoted to mathematics. Yet it is he who contributes more than
any one else to the introduction of Newton to
the French public, and who emphasizes the
essential merit of Newton: namely, that he
refused to maintain anything that was not immediately, constantly, and exactly verifiable by
the facts. The first works of Montesquieu are
monographs on physics and physiology for
the Academy of Bordeaux. Diderot always
had the liveliest and the most penetrating
curiosity about all the natural sciences. He
followed courses in anatomy and physiology,
and for three years took the course of the
chemist, Rouelle. He helped to create the
popularity of the anatomical wax models of

Mlle Biheron; he composed the important *Elements of Physiology*. When J.-J. Rousseau decides to further his education at the Charmettes, he learns astronomy and medicine together with his mathematics. He has left us, as a sort of summary of his readings, a very long work on the *Elements of Chemistry*. D'Holbach is a reputable chemist who translates half a dozen works on chemistry, metallurgy, and so on. We have mentioned the treatise on experiments of the philosopher, Deslandes. The works of Condillac, Turgot, and Condorcet indicate *passim* that they were familiar with the most important contemporary works on physics, chemistry, and natural history.

The great scientists or even the modest scientists of the time rapidly acquired celebrity with the general public. In almost all circles one reads the *Spectacle of Nature* by Pluche, the *History of Insects* by Réaumur, the works on physics by the abbé Nollet. Buffon in particular enjoys a prodigious reputation. For all those who are not scientists, he is "the Pliny and the Aristotle of France." Ten poets eulogize him; the king makes him a count. A statue is erected to Voltaire during his own lifetime; but Buffon is similarly honored, and the most renowned poets vie in suggesting an inscription that will be worthy of his genius. Ferney, Clarens, the rue Plâtrière, where Rousseau lives, are all places of pilgrimage; but so is Montbard. When Buffon dies, Montbard receives his mortal remains with all the homage due to a hero. For a year a mortuary chapel stands, with all its tapers aglow, on the hill that faces the château. "One approached his study," says a contemporary, "as though it were a temple, of which his old valet was the guardian, and his son the pontiff."

The delight in experimental science was universal: a hundred witnesses attest the fact. "Works on physics are so warmly welcomed by the present-day public that one is always sure of delighting it when one composes a work on that subject. . . . To-day the study of natural history is the most popular of all." Even the heroes of novels give themselves up without reserve to the "mania for natural history." "The superficially learned element of contemporary society has withdrawn from scholarly erudition to devote itself to the sciences." For this superficially learned element, as well as for serious people, there is the pleasure of visiting the various zoölogical and botanical collections. That zoölogical collection known variously as the Cabinet of the King, or the Garden of the King, or the Garden of Plants, became famous, thanks to Buffon; but there were many others. Dezallier d'Argenville in 1780 indicates sixty-two that have been but recently opened. The prince de Condé is very proud of the one that is directed by Valmost de Bomare. Besides, certain very popular courses are being given. Valmont de Bomare begins his in 1757; he is forced to divide it into two sections in 1769, because of its popularity. Sigaud de la Fond, Brisson, Maybert de Gouvest give courses in experimental physics in Paris. There are similar courses even in the provinces. Even society ladies yearn to perfect themselves in the sciences of the Nollets, the Réaumurs, and the Buffons. In the seventies Deparcieux comes from Paris every year to the château of Brienne to give a course of six weeks or two months "for the ladies." There are hundreds of treatises, monographs, dictionaries of physics and of natural history; but there are also many works that are compendiums, manuals, lessons, courses "for the use of society people," "for general use," or even "for young ladies."

The study of the experimental sciences

penetrates academic circles, though rather timidly. For a long time, one year or perhaps several months of the two years devoted to philosophy had been given up to "general and practical physics." But it was only a branch of scholastic philosophy; moreover, the philosophy professor was also the physics professor. After the expulsion of the Jesuits in 1762, it becomes a rather generally established rule that there is to be a physics professor as well as a philosophy professor. Of course the two years of philosophy do not form a part of the regular curriculum; they are taken by only half, and often by only a quarter, of the student body. But in the teaching of physics there is an increasing tendency to restrict "general physics," which is merely the metaphysics of matter, in favor of "practical" or experimental physics. In a great number of colleges, the curriculum includes a study of the treatises that Nollet composed for pedagogical purposes; apparatus is bought, and is often found included in the inventories of the time. Often enough, it is true, the physical instruction is weak or even ridiculous, and the "laboratories" are rudimentary. But the theorists of pedagogy and the masters of boarding schools are far more advanced. "No more nursery tales," says one, "no more fables of La Fontaine; at the age of two to four years the child is to study Buffon, at four years, physics." "At eight years," says another, "experimental physics." A certain *Treatise on the Education of Women* devotes Volumes III and IV to experimental physics. And the abbé Fromageot details for Mme de Sainte-Valérie, first mistress of the schoolgirls of the Abbey of Port-Royal, the reasons that induced him to include experimental science in his program: "I included natural history and physics as essential in education; I regarded them as two inexhaustible sources of pleasure, and as the most certain antidotes against boredom and idleness."

The scientists and the philosophers, even the journalists and the pedagogues have given more serious reasons than those of Fromageot to justify the study of experimental physics and natural history. They saw therein not merely a remedy for boredom but a source of discipline for the mind, a moral force. "The study of physics," says the philosopher Deslandes, "is one of the noblest and most virtuous occupations of the human mind. . . . He who, conscious of the dignity of his being and

possessing his soul in tranquillity, loves to consider the works of nature and to analyze them
carefully passes his days in the most agreeable
manner because his pleasures are pure, wholesome, and not subject to the bitter reproaches
that sensuality brings in its train." Deslandes
was a philosopher, but Bertrand was a pastor,
and he speaks in the same tone: "I do not hesitate to say that morality and natural history
are, together with revelation, the most important objects of human knowledge." And
it is the prudent and not overserious *Mercury* which in 1781 intonates this hymn: "A
genuine naturalist is a man who, tormented by
the love of truth and conceiving of no other
happiness than that of knowing it, seeks it in
labors of every sort; who, yearning to inter-
rogate Nature, courageously confronts all the
obstacles that might conceal her from him.
Neither the rapidity of torrents, nor the width
of rivers, nor the towering aspect of the most
inaccessible crags, nor the encounter of the
unchained elements, can arrest his progress."

The study of the experimental sciences becomes almost a new religion, with its renun-
ciations and its ecstasies. "The knowledge of
nature," says Buc'hoz, who is not a philos-

opher, "is, so to speak, the forerunner of celes-
tial voluptuousness; once one has enjoyed it,
one walks in light and one leads a life as delightful as though one were in a terrestrial
paradise." One dreams of erecting temples to
this god and to his devotees: these temples,
as often as not, will be only literary affairs and
composed of verses. Voltaire and Bonnet ask
men of letters to seek "inspiration in so worthy a subject." Chénier begins his *Hermes*,
and Lebrun-Pindare a poem on *Nature*.
Diderot and the abbé Saury urge the construction of more tangible edifices: "It would be
worthy of a great prince to erect to nature a
palace in which would be included all the objects deserving the attention of naturalists.
. . . What a spectacle that would be: all the
objects that the hand of the Omnipotent has
scattered over the surface of the earth, exhib-
ited in a single place!" M. Viel undertook to
convert this "spectacle" into a reality and published the project of a vast monument to be
devoted to the glory and to the teaching of
natural history. One will stand before this
monument with a spirit transformed by the
experimental sciences, delivered from the
past, prepared for the future. "Nature," rimes
Fabre d'Eglantine:

Nature, I feel, is that beloved art
That gives solace and strength alike to mind
    and heart,
And sunders all the chains of prejudice.

One might believe that only the philosophers are occupied in denouncing these
"chains of prejudice." But many others who
are not philosophers use the same language,
and one can place in juxtaposition the convictions and the hopes of Condorcet, who is an
Encyclopedist, Roucher, who is a "sentimental soul" and a poet, Nollet and Leclerc, who
are respectively abbé and canon. "The most
important of the benefits of science are, perhaps, the destroying of prejudices and the up-
lifting of human intelligence. . . . The sage
will patiently wait for observation to bring
him the fateful lever that is to overturn utterly the edifice of error and to bury its unfortunate architect under its ruins. Then the
stupid errors that debase the human race and
deliver it, bound hand and foot, to superstition will seek refuge in flight, and will never
reappear." Finally the eulogies of Buffon
written by his secretary, Humbert-Bazile, and
by Condorcet map out an entire program of
"positive philosophy": "Living in a century
in which the human mind, struggling with its

chains, loosened them all and even cast off
some . . . , M. de Buffon appeared to have
taken no part in the general movement. But
perhaps he thought that the best means of destroying errors in metaphysics and in ethics
was to multiply the truths of observation in
the natural sciences; that instead of actively
opposing the ignorant and the stubborn it was
necessary to inspire them with the desire to
seek instruction."

CHAPTER III

THE POSITIVE SPIRIT

FACTS AND THE LESSONS DRAWN FROM FACTS

Historical note.—Diderot (1713-1784) was born at Langres in 1713; his father was a rich cutler. After brilliantly concluding his academic studies Diderot eked out a scanty living by tutoring and other expedients in order to continue his studies in accordance with his own preferences. He published a translation of the *Essay on Merit and Virtue* by Shaftesbury, a rather anodyne performance, then certain *Philosophical Thoughts,* which were much less so. Denounced as an atheist by his curate and the police commissioner of his district, he was imprisoned for three months in the château of Vincennes after the publication of the *Letter on the Blind for the Use of Those Who See* (1749). Then he published anonymously and without being molested the *Thoughts on the Interpretation of Nature* (1754) ; *On the Sufficiency of Natural Religion* (1770) ; *The Conversation of a Philosopher with the Duchesse de * * ** (1776) ; *Essay on the Life of Seneca the Philosopher*. Certain unpublished manuscripts were published posthumously (among these is the *Dream of d'Alembert*). He busied himself with literary criticism, writing the *Eulogy of Richardson* (1761) and the *Reflections on Terence* (1762) ; and he also expounded various poetic and dramatic theories (*Conversa-*

149

tions on the Natural Son, Discourses on Dramatic Poetry, Paradox on the Comedian). He attempted to apply his theories on the stage by composing mediocre dramas (*The Natural Son,* 1757, and *The Paterfamilias,* 1758, the last enjoying a fair share of success). His novels were published after his death: *The Nun* and *Jacques the Fatalist* in 1796, *The Nephew of Rameau* in 1823. His art criticism, contained in the summaries of the *Salons* that he wrote for the *Literary Correspondence of Grimm,* was published posthumously.

The great task of his life was the publication of the *Encyclopedia.* Certain Parisian publishers desired to publish a translation of the *Cyclopedia* of the Englishman, Chambers. Diderot, whom they approached in the matter, conceived the idea of organizing an original work which was to be a vast classified dictionary of human knowledge. He became associated in the enterprise with d'Alembert, secured the collaboration of Voltaire, J.-J. Rousseau, Montesquieu, Turgot, and others. The first volume appeared in 1751 with a *Preliminary Discourse* by d'Alembert. We shall consider later the obstacles that the authorities opposed to its publication. This dictionary, which was completed in 1766, contained 17 folio volumes, 5 supplementary volumes, and 11 volumes of plates.

The sensistic philosophy.—The classical spirit came upon Cartesian rationalism and found therein a source of justification and new strength. Now experimentation has practically no rôle in the philosophy of Descartes; the only sort of demonstration that is valid is rational evidence. To understand the rise of mercury in the tube of Torricelli and the

nature of the vacuum it is useless to experiment; it is quite sufficient to reason about the matter. For a long time this Cartesianism appeared to be an audacious and dangerous doctrine. Yet, after 1740 it is scarcely anything more than a historical remembrance; it has been replaced by a philosophy of observation, the sensism of Locke.

Descartes says: "Let us put our trust in reason; it is infallible." But why is it infallible, any more so, for example, than the syllogisms of the Scholastics? Is it not necessary to justify it? "I accept as true," continues Descartes, "only what I know to be true." But what does "to know" signify? What is the nature of this perception of truth? Is it such a simple and certain operation after all? What is evident for Descartes is not at all so for a child, a savage, a fanatic. It becomes necessary therefore to examine the rights of reason, to study the mechanism of knowledge, in short, to judge judgment itself by precise analysis. That is what Locke proposed to do in observing the formation and the function of "human understanding."

The results of the analysis are important. To furnish a foundation for the rights of reason, Descartes assumes without examination and without proof that it is immutable and universal. It constitutes a perfect reality in all men and it is "innate" from the very outset. In the child, in the uncultured man, and in the savage it is the same as in Descartes; only it is dormant, not as yet utilized. Now Locke does not believe that all the ideas of reason are innate. Those which seem to us the most necessary are often not only unknown but even contradicted by the actual facts. Children, idiots, savages have no idea of God; by certain savages it is deemed pious to eat one's enemies. Let us therefore examine our intellectual faculties at closer range; we shall see that the child has no intellectual faculty, or at least that he has only certain vague aptitudes. He experiences sensations; he remembers them; and it is by the memory of these experiences that he acquires what was not at all innate: attention, comparison, judgment, reasoning power.

Conclusion: before constructing a theory of the world that is to be based on reason, one must obtain a clear conception of just what the mind is. We learn to know it by observation, and observation reveals to us that the reasoning faculties of the mind are formed by experience. In a word, philosophy consists less of reasoning than of observing facts and the relation between facts. This philosophy of facts, *sensistic* philosophy (because it is based upon the facts of sensation) exercised the profoundest influence throughout the eighteenth century. We have mentioned the fact that the *Essay on Human Understanding* was already known by the end of the seventeenth century. In the eighteenth, Locke is not only known but almost universally admired. Voltaire eulogizes him enthusiastically on twenty different occasions. All the philosophers admire him as wholeheartedly: d'Argens, whose *Philosophy of Good Sense* is the philosophy of Locke, whose *Index* to the *Jewish Letters* contains a page of references to Locke (only half a page is devoted to Gassendi); Vauvenargues; Deslandes; and even those who are not philosophers, like Father Buffier. After 1750 the enthusiasm does not abate. Diderot echoes Voltaire: "Locke's philosophy, compared with that of Descartes or with that of Malebranche, is history compared to fiction." Rousseau, who studies the *Essay* at the Charmettes, constantly recalls Locke in his *Emile*, D'Holbach refers to the "profound Locke." For Saint-Lambert he is "the wisest and the most enlightened of all the teachers of

the human race." Helvétius admits the simi-
larity of his own opinions to those of Locke;
and in point of fact he has contented himself
with applying Locke's method with clumsy
literalness.

There was moreover a "French Locke,"
whose influence heightened that of Locke. The
Treatise on Sensations of Condillac (1754)
gained rapid popularity. He followed Locke's
method in thoroughgoing fashion. He desired to know if the "faculties of the soul,"
if the forms of our intelligence, were innate
or whether they had not been slowly formed
by the experience of the senses. But he went
further than Locke and he was more methodical. Locke had not always been a realist; he
had expounded a system of metaphysics and
a religion that he called "rational," but in
which observation and experience counted for
nothing. Condillac is very sincerely spiritual-
istic and pious, but he never speaks of religion; that is not the object of his philosophy.
Locke does not believe in the "innate faculties"; yet he speaks of primitive aptitudes.
For Condillac nothing is innate. There is
nothing in the mind at birth but the animal
aptitude for experiencing sensations and the
very general aptitude (which is bestowed by

God and which distinguishes us from the animals) for profiting thereby, not by the development of an internal force, but by the lessons acquired through experience. Condillac intends to study the progress of this experience. At birth the human mind is like a statue, a mere form. Let us bestow life upon the statue; let us give it the sense of smell. By the experience that it will have of odors, pleasant and repugnant, the statue will acquire attention, comparison, memory, judgment, generalization, and so on. The study of the other senses and of the collaboration of the senses will permit us to understand well how all our faculties are acquired, and "externally acquired, by the influence of realities placed outside ourselves." "It is," concludes the philosopher Höffding, "the most thoroughgoing effort that has ever been made to derive everything from experience."

Let us add (the fact has not been brought out clearly enough) that Condillac did not content himself with appealing to inner observation, which after all retains an abstract character because one "assumes" the various states of mind of the statue or of the child. He was not only concerned with mathematics; he was keenly interested in natural history.

He wrote a *Treatise on Animals*, directed against Buffon, precisely because he accused Buffon of explaining animals by a preconceived system rather than by accurate observation. He bases his views (rather diffidently, indeed) upon the experiences of the blind man of Cheselden, upon experiments on the localization of pain, on the illusions of the senses, on harmonic resonances; he is on the road to experimental psychology. Condillac was the friend and even the companion of the eighteenth century philosophers, who greatly admired him. Voltaire considers that he is equal to Locke. Rousseau places him "among the greatest logicians and the profoundest metaphysicians of his century." Diderot thinks that he is "clearer than Locke." He is constantly being cited directly or indirectly in the works of the abbé de Prades, Helvétius, d'Holbach, Robinet, Delisle de Sales, Beaurieu, and various others.

Another step remained to be taken, however, before philosophy could be solidly bound to the experimental sciences, which enjoyed such a complete triumph after 1750; Diderot took the step. If the understanding is formed within us by the sensations, the sensations themselves are either material or in close dependence upon matter, that is to say, upon the nerves and the brain. Now in physics and in natural history one experiments upon matter, and it is by virtue of these experiments that one discovers the solutions of various problems. Why should philosophy not attempt the same method? Diderot firmly believes that it is possible and even necessary. "Everything in us is subject to experimentation," he writes to Mlle Voland. And the *Thoughts on the Interpretation of Nature*, the *Letter on the Blind,* that on the *Deaf and Dumb*, and also certain works that he really composes for his own delectation clearly present the method and carry it forward to its extreme consequences. In order to understand sensation, one must first understand life in its most elementary forms: "One must begin by classifying all beings, the inert molecule, if there be any, the living molecule, the microscopic animal, the animal-plant, the animal, man." In the animal and in man the sensations depend upon the organs: it will be necessary then to observe the formation of these organs, to follow the experiences that create therein maladies such as blindness, deafness, hysteria, intoxication; even to provoke these experiences if need be. In a word, the philosopher must base his work on physiology, natural history, medicine. The best philosophers will be men who are blind from birth and who are capable of comparing their experiences with those of normal men, or else full-fledged doctors with a thorough grounding in anatomy and physiology. And we shall be able to arrive at an explanation of life that will no longer be rationalistic and abstract, but materialistic, that is to say, supported entirely by experiences which are self-sufficient without the intervention of an incomprehensible and consequently arbitrary spiritual principle. A being is an aggregate of elementary beings; it is perfected by the very action of life. "The organs produce one's needs and, reciprocally, one's needs produce the organs"; these needs produce and develop the so-called spiritual organs, the pretended faculties of the soul, which evolve, vary, change, exactly like the material organs, that is to say, which "are nothing outside of themselves." Philosophy is only a branch of science, of experimental science, of the science of matter.

The other philosophers, whether materialistic or not, did not have Diderot's sagacity. They had less interest in physiology or medicine; and it seemed to them more expedient to reason than to study reality. All, however, realized the worth of experience and the value of the experimental methods, which they even practiced on occasion. Often they declared in favor of observation and experimentation as against the "systems"; they preferred the scientists, resigned to the "modesty of experimentation," to the "systematizers." In the "quarrel of the systems" which we have already described, they delivered the most telling blows against the "abstract philosophers." Voltaire praises experimentation more than he practices it; he is hardly capable of a consistent philosophy. But Helvétius declares that every system "crumbles even as it is being constructed, if it be not erected upon the unshakable foundation of facts and of experimentation." He wishes to establish a system of ethics as he would a system of experimental physics. It is quite certain that he promised more than he fulfilled. But he *does* seek to base his research upon facts, upon hundreds of facts. Many of them, indeed, are doubtful or false; but he has borrowed them from the only guarantors at his disposal, from Buffon, from those who have spoken of the Marianas, the Chiriguanos, Pegu, the Caribbeans, and so forth, and finally from the anthropology and the ethnography of his time. He knows, and he also cites, the works of chemists, doctors, and naturalists. If he reasons badly, he often reasons upon the facts or rather upon what men considered to be the facts at the time. D'Holbach has the same scruples: "Man must constantly have recourse to physics and experience in all his researches." Of course he seeks other props without suspecting it. But he calls upon anatomical and medical arguments, upon the experiments or the observations of La Peyronie, Bartolin, and Willes on lethargy, trepanation, the proportions of the brain, nourishment. He cites, as does Helvétius, the observations of travelers; he makes an attempt at comparative mythology. He wishes to be scientific.

If he is no more successful therein than Helvétius, it is partly his own fault, but it is also partly the fault of his time. The facts of which Helvétius and d'Holbach must needs avail themselves are sometimes as accurate as these: that certain peoples have no articulate language; that flour in a state of fermentation engenders worms; that the flesh of certain sick persons may be transformed, suddenly and completely, into lice and fleas. These are errors which give rise to other errors. Helvétius and d'Holbach had faulty instruments; with them they were able to accomplish only imperfect or mediocre work. But their intentions were in accordance with the experimental philosophy of their critic, Taine.

History—literature.—The same realistic spirit is to be found in history, and occasionally in literature proper, in the drama, the novel, and descriptive poetry. Throughout the seventeenth century, and at the beginning of the eighteenth, history was not to be distinguished from eloquence, panegyric, or the diverting and moralizing novel. It is practically impossible to establish a line of demarcation between what the authors call "history" and what they call "anecdote" or "historical novel." Toward the end of the eighteenth century, Mably, studying the "manner of writing history," will still wonder if it be wise to "plunge into the study of our diplomas, our ancient formulas, and our capitularies, and to groan under this enormous litter of documents, calculated to make the most intrepid and persevering scholar recoil in terror." A number of historians do not concern themselves with this "litter," and until the very end of the century they continue to apply the rules of rhetoric rather than those of historical research and criticism. Voltaire, however, believed that historical truth could be ascertained only after a patient study of the facts. In the composition of his *Century of Louis XIV* he was not content with having new ideas and writing the history of a nation and of thought, rather than that of a prince and conquering strategy; he wished to obtain exact information. He questioned contemporaries as to the deeds that he narrated; he procured numberless unpublished memoirs, or extracts from memoirs, and authentic documents; he consulted the archives of the government. Whenever he could do so, he employed firsthand sources. The *Essay on the Customs and the Spirit of Nations* is the summary of an immense and patient investigation, a prodigious effort of research and organization. It is no longer a "System" or mere "Reflections"; it is really an orderly exposition of the facts, of whatever knowledge one could possibly have between 1740 and 1760 of what had actually happened in the world. And if Voltaire was the only one who had the genius requisite to organize historical research and to endow it with life, he was not the only one in the eighteenth century to attempt to found history upon exact research. Before him the Benedictines had for a long time been plunged in the study of the "litter" of old manuscripts. The Academy of Inscriptions had suddenly lost interest in drawing up inscriptions dedicated to the glory of Louis XIV. Toward 1700 it had become an assemblage of scholars engaged in making a minute study of monuments, texts, documentary history. In order to determine the origin and the progress of various civilizations, Voltaire and other scholars (whose researches are summed up in the *Encyclopedia*) study the history of writing, languages, monuments, texts. Voyages and explorations of every sort multiply these documents; with the discovery of the ruins of Pompeii and Herculaneum, a real and living Rome replaces the oratorical and bookish Rome of the colleges. And the abbé de Barthélemy's *Voyage of Young Anacharsis* (1788), which was one of the illustrious books of the end of the eighteenth century, is a compendium of the learned researches not only of the abbé but also of those of other archæologists or historians. It is really a *Telemachus* in which historical curiosity has taken the place of moral teaching.

History pervades all things, real history, or perhaps more exactly the historical spirit, the desire to know just what the past was. The *Bucolics* of Chénier do not constitute a new literary type. But from Fontenelle to Gessner the "idyl" is concerned with being "gallant" or "simple" or "ingenious" or "naïve," but never with being exactly Greek or Latin. The *Bucolics*, however, are a masterpiece of erudition as well as a masterpiece of grace and harmony. One may say that Chénier read all the Greek texts; and he read them with the commentaries of the scholars of his time, and first-rate scholars like Guys and Brunck. It is in the eighteenth century that literary criticism often becomes literary history and that judgments on taste become the history of taste. All the literature of the Middle Ages emerges from obscurity; one finds delight in "chivalry," the "troubadours," Gothic architecture and literature, in everything that recalls the "good old times" and "the old language." For example, the *Library of Romances* (1775-1789), which is a rather popular publication, gives forty extracts from the romances of the Middle Ages in its two hundred volumes. It has been found possible to draw up a bibliography of more than a hundred works in which there appears the desire, often quite clearly expressed, to compose the history of literature and no longer merely to catalogue it and to judge it. Moreover, everything now has its "history." Deslandes, for example, in 1756 composes his *Critical History of Philosophy*, Sevérien a *History of Modern Philosophies* (1760-1773), a *History of Ancient Philosophies* (1770), a *History of the Progress of the Human Mind in the Exact Sciences* (1766-1778), Mentucla a *History of Mathematics* (1758). And similarly one could cite many histories of sciences, of discoveries, of legislation, of customs. These histories are confused, ill-informed, uninspired, but they are really histories, descriptions of the past, in which a conscious effort is made no longer to give free rein to one's imagination, but to describe facts, texts, monuments.

This realistic spirit penetrates literature itself. The taste for realism is not classical, at least not before La Bruyère. The remark has often been made that the stage has no scenery, that we do not know whether Hermione and Andromache are brunette or blonde, and that we learn nothing about the personal appearance of the princesse de Clèves except that she is blonde. This indifference persists for a long time in the eighteenth century. In all the celebrated romances of Mme de Tencin or of the abbé Prévost, one would seek in vain the details that conjure up definite faces and bodies. We know that a heroine like the Marianne of Marivaux or the Manon of the abbé Prévost may have a mischievous air, a fine eye, little feet, a charming face, a soft glance, grace, charms, everything, in short, that would make us eager to know her, and yet there is nothing that would enable us to see her as she really is. The drama until about 1750 remains as conventional as that of the seventeenth century. The stage is still encumbered with benches for spectators; the Greeks, Romans, or Turks wear wigs or hoop petticoats and slaves wear most elaborate diamonds.

Little by little a general though not universal transformation takes place. There are lifelike physical portraits in the *Gil Blas* of Lesage and in the *Memoirs of the Comte de Grammont* of Hamilton. In Voltaire we find not genuine portraits but at least expressive silhouettes. We see the Cunégonde of *Candide* with her high color, fresh, plump, enticing; we also have a really vivid image of Mlle de Kerkabon of the *Ingenuous Man*. Toward 1750 the English novels of Fielding and Richardson reveal a bolder realism. These novels are sublime, according to Diderot;

they represent the image not of selected, embellished, disguised life, but life as it is and in its every phase. "I know the house of the Harlowes as though it were my own; the abode of my father is not more familiar to me than that of Grandison." And he wished to depict persons and things with the veracity of a Richardson. He has given the most precise definition that we possess of the "tale," that is to say, of the realistic novel. Indicate a wart on the face of Jupiter, a smallpox scar on that of Venus, and you will have your own neighbors instead of an unapproachable Jupiter and Venus. *Jacques the Fatalist* and the *Nephew of Rameau* in particular endeavor to give us portraits in which there are warts and scars. One might also find this same fidelity in description, the sketch of a vein or the exact appearance of a house, in the *Modern Héloïse* and the *Émile* of Rousseau and in other novels (although this realism remains timid and cautious). On the stage toward 1750-1760 the peasants of the comic opera are clad in veritable peasant garb, with simple dresses, aprons, wooden shoes. Mlle Clairon wears Oriental garments to represent Roxane, chains to represent the slave, Electra. The benches on the stage disappear in 1759. The drama is very often a melodrama, that is to say, that for the convention of tragic dignity is substituted another, that of caverns, gibbets, and death's-heads. But still Diderot presents the theory of scenic variety and tries to put it into practice. He desires to have "tableaux," that is to say, settings and the kind of acting that will give us the illusion of actually living with the personages presented and not merely of being in "a palace" or in "a square." The drama is "middle-class" or even "plebeian": that is to say, it has as its heroes peasants or vinegar-merchants; it depicts or makes an effort to depict customs. Literature no longer proposes to remain faithful only to universal "nature" and "reason": it begins to describe a nook of Switzerland, a Bohemian quarter, the house of a respectable *paterfamilias* who lives under Louis XV, or that of a vintager of Suresnes.

Education.—This taste for reality becomes so pronounced toward 1760 that it tends to transform education, which has so obstinately resisted transformation. We have shown how, throughout the eighteenth century, the pedagogues had remained faithful to the principles that extended back a century and more. They thought that their methods were eternally good, that the qualities of an able mind do not change with the times, and that there is no need of bringing about changes in the pedagogic devices that form this mind. Little by little, however, a certain uneasiness penetrates and becomes increasingly precise; later it expresses itself in wrath and sarcasm. The colleges teach Latin, nothing but Latin: they prepare their students to compose and to recite discourses, odes, elegies. But what has one to do with Latin, with discourses, and with elegies when one is to be a captain, a cloth-merchant, a manufacturer of stockings, or an agriculturist? Even France needs merchants and agriculturists more than she does procurators, lawyers, or theologians. Education should adequately train Frenchmen who are to have other duties than those of paying fine compliments or making elegant bows. Education should be realistic and no longer scholastic or even merely academic.

The great master of this reform movement was of course Rousseau. *Émile* was famous from the very outset and its lessons were sometimes followed with stupid confidence. There were certain disciples of Rousseau who left their children in the fields all day so that they might live "according to nature." But Rousseau converted many sensible people also; he taught them certain valid principles. To instruct a child is really to teach him how to live. Now life does not concern itself with what is in books, with synecdoche and catachresis, with the sublimity of words and the sublimity of thoughts; it is composed of experiences and of struggles which have nothing in common with those academic competitions in which a "pupil-tribune" triumphs over a "pupil-emperor" because he has cited Vergil more aptly or because he has constructed his syllogisms more skillfully. Education should consequently be more realistic. Émile is to be put in constant contact with objects and persons; he is to be taught geography by walks, natural history by object lessons, the ideas of violence, of justice, and of prudence by being subjected to violence, injustice and imprudence, and so on. In the second place, the important thing is to develop not the memory or even the ingenuity of the child, but his judgment. The merit of a mind is to be measured not by its skill in applying the ideas of others but by its aptitude in forming its own ideas judiciously. The child will have to live not among Greeks, Romans, orators and college teachers, but among men who will pervert and exploit him if he be not able to judge men and to understand reality.

This doctrine of the *Émile* is essential not only because it is in great part judicious, but because it has had converts and influence since the eighteenth century. It is not original, however. What is original with Rousseau is an idea that represents an obvious error: it is to the effect that in every child, provided he be sheltered from influences that might possibly pervert him, nature is always and perfectly good and that one has only to let nature function. But this particular idea is almost always left to Rousseau. It is true that theorists (like Guillard de Beaurieu) carry it to a ridiculous extreme; but pedagogues in general confine themselves to his other ideas: realistic, practical education and the formation of the judgment. Now before the *Émile* one finds these ideas in certain authors who are widely read, in the *Education of Children* by Locke, in the treatises of Crousaz, Morelly, and others. After the *Émile* these concepts become mere commonplaces. One could give a long list of the pedagogues who not only demand reforms in education, but reforms which are to renovate it entirely.

The problem is definitely presented in 1762. The order of the Jesuits is suppressed in France; they are expelled from the hundred and twenty colleges that they have been directing. It is necessary to replace them; and for that very reason it becomes necessary to replace their method. Conferences are organized on a great scale. La Chalotais, President Rolland, Guyton de Morveau discuss and propose; many others, including philosophers, educators, boarding school teachers, imitate them. Of course they are not in mutual agreement; there are bold, and there are timid, innovators. But all, or almost all, favor practical, realistic instruction: the sciences, object lessons, history, French.

To consider one example: It is true that French does not definitely triumph over Latin. Latin remains the essential subject almost everywhere, except in the case of certain private schools of which we have only the prospectuses. But pedagogical theorists, who are very numerous, discuss and condemn Latin, sometimes with sarcasm and indignation. From the first half of the century there is a Latin question; the tyranny of Latin studies is assailed by almost all the philosophers, Diderot, d'Alembert, Duclos, La Condamine, and Voltaire himself, in spite of his triumphs in Latin at college. A Swiss "pedant" and pedagogue, Crousaz, combats in behalf of French and scientific studies side by side with novelists like Prévost, society people like the comte de Tressan, poets like Béranger, "sentimental souls" like L.-S. Mercier or Bernardin de Saint-Pierre. They even have certain professors as their allies, men like the Jesuit Berland, the abbé Gédoyn, Father Navarre, Father Papon, principal at Lyons, Mathias, principal at Langres, and others. In actual practice, and that after all is the important thing, French now has an important rôle. Not everywhere, let us observe; and even when it is taught, it is often negligently taught. But toward 1760, nevertheless, among the discourses delivered at the opening term or at the distribution of prizes, among the programs of public exercises, there appear discourses, programs, exercises in French. They become the rule rather than the exception toward 1780. Rhetoric is taught in French almost universally toward 1770, and so is physics. Toward 1780 philosophy is not being taught in Latin so frequently as before. There are prizes for proficiency in French rhetoric in almost all the colleges of the Oratorians from

1764 or 1770, and in the majority of colleges
after 1780. Cicero, Vergil, Horace, and Quintilian no longer shut the door upon Bossuet,
Massillon, Boileau, and Molière. For the cult
of the past is substituted the study of the
present and of almost contemporary authors.

Realistic politics.—It would be quite surprising if this realistic spirit were to enlist
even the colleges and yet have no influence
upon the theorists of politics. Taine and
Tocqueville have scoffingly called them "theorists of the study, architects of clouds." But
in reality Taine and Tocqueville were "theorists of the study," whereas most of the political reformers whom they derided had more
or less extensive practical experience. Fénelon
administered his diocese; Vauban traveled ex-
tensively in the provinces in the course of
his engineering work; Boisguilbert was the
executive of a bailiwick; Montesquieu was
a councilor, then the president of the Parliament of Bordeaux; Helvétius, the son of a
doctor, was a farmer-general, a squire resid-
ing on his own estates and administering
them; Voltaire built up a great fortune and
made a rich and industrious district of a little
village on poor soil; Turgot was the *intendant*
of Limoges, and later minister; Mably was

the secretary of the Cardinal de Tencin and prepared negotiations and treaties; the economists were horticulturalists, secretaries of *intendants*, or *intendants* themselves; Rousseau, who came from a city where every one dabbled in politics, disentangled the affairs of Mme de Warens, or attempted to do so, and he was secretary to an ambassador; d'Holbach carefully looked after his vast fortune and his estates. Of those whose interest was chiefly theoretical we can name only Diderot, Raynal, and Condorcet. And the concern for reality appears very clearly in the works of even these men.

Montesquieu belonged to the *Club of the Entresol* in which were discussed the *history* of treaties, the *history* of states-general and of parliaments, the *history* of commerce. And his *Spirit of the Laws* is, or at least aims to be, a *history* of the laws; instead of judging them or reasoning about them according to the systems of natural right or rational law, he establishes what the laws are in the light of reality. The conclusion is that these laws are good when they realize not equity and justice in themselves, but that type of equity or justice that is compatible with the climate, the habitat, and the customs of a given group of men.

One may say that Voltaire has no political theory, no system. He has only partially developed ideas and these ideas are constantly a reaction against immediate realities, against perfectly definite abuses and in view of practical reforms. D'Holbach writes two "Discourses" or chapters in order to demonstrate that no form of government is equally appropriate for all peoples, no legislation for all men, and that one must distinguish between varying times and places. Undoubtedly Mably is a rationalistic philosopher: he is persuaded that a good political system should tend to realize certain ideas and that there will be no solidly established society so long as the prevailing political system does not observe justice and the rational laws of social equilibrium *per se*. Yet he knows perfectly well that "however profound a given political system may be, it will never be as crafty as human passion; were it only as crafty, it would be less stubborn in its desires and less attentive to the daily detail of its operations." Consequently one must take human passion into account; likewise one must study the object lessons of history. And the ideas of Mably are founded, or are intended to be founded, upon facts: upon the decadence of Spain, the history of

Florence, the customs of Georgia, the history
of the plebs at Rome and of the English people, upon the revolutions of Sweden, upon the
history of the Quakers, and so forth. He reproaches Montesquieu for forcing the laws
(and reason and justice themselves as a consequence) to change according to the climate
and the form of government. The dream of
the future in the *Historical Sketch of the Human Mind* of Condorcet is the dream of an
international society (or something of that
sort), ruled by a council of philosophers; and
it is, if you will, only a dream. But Condorcet
is, as he says, a disciple of Locke and of
Hume. He believes in observation, in experimentation, in the necessity of resigning oneself to ignorance in certain matters. With the
economists he arrives at one of the first results
of observation in the sciences: differentiation.
In general history and politics he creates political economy and he outlines sociology.

Moreover, all our political thinkers of the
eighteenth century have always carefully distinguished between the theory that is a mere
convenience and auxiliary of thought, and the
practical consequences that must be drawn
therefrom. They construct systems indeed; but
the ruin of a scientific system does not neces-

sarily entail the destruction of the discoveries founded upon observation and experience. The *Social Contract* of Rousseau is merely a mental exercise, an effort at organization of ideas. It is the *Contract* that is generally cited whenever an attempt is made to prove that the political philosophy of the eighteenth century substituted abstract logic for realistic politics. And indeed it is not doubtful that certain revolutionaries desired to carry out the ideas of the *Contract*. But this *Contract* never represented the author's ultimate idea of political theory. It was to form part of a *Treatise on Political Institutions*, but Rousseau never said that it was to constitute the most important part of the treatise. Rousseau never spoke of the *Contract* as being a particularly important work; and his contemporaries before the Revolution seem to have considered it as no more than a species of philosophical entertainment. For every allusion to the *Contract* there are ten allusions to the *Modern Héloïse* and to *Émile*.

When Rousseau desires to pass from speculation to practice, he draws up for the Poles or for the Corsicans certain projects in which there is no mention of a "pact," a "state religion," or dictatorial measures for the protection of the pact. The other political theorists pursue exactly the same method. To take only one example: not one of these precursors of the Revolution, these defenders of "natural rights," thought that France might be organized as a democracy or even as a constitutional monarchy. Voltaire repeated on many different occasions that "democracy seems to be appropriate only for a very small country"; and besides it must be "appropriately situated." Together with a professed "love for the people" he had a hatred for the "populace"; and at times these two words seem to have an identical meaning for him. Rousseau believes that democracy is possible in a small state like Geneva, perhaps in a pastoral community such as one may find in Corsica; but not in Poland or in France. The *Social System* of d'Holbach, distinguishing at great length between "people" and "populace," condemns democracy, equality and revolutions. Mably indeed goes so far as to suggest the ultimate suppression of landed property, but this dream of equality is modified by all sorts of prudent provisos that hardly suggest communism. He fears the "degraded multitude" and withdraws the legislative power from it. He demands the separation of the powers, the subordina-

tion of the executive power to the legislative
power. He concludes that "pure democracy
would be an excellent type of government
in a land with good morals, but detestable
in a land with morals like ours." Condorcet
indeed demands a definition of the "rights of
man" and insists upon equality; but on the
eve of the Revolution he would deprive of
all political rights those whom he calls "pas-
sive citizens," the non-proprietors. The other
philosophers are even more prudent. For L.-
S. Mercier democracy is "the worst of all possible governments." Diderot, who does not
concern himself overmuch with politics, considers that democracy is possible only in Holland or in Switzerland; like Voltaire he
favors "an enlightened despot." The *Encyclopedia*, which reflects their opinions rather
exactly, is more or less audacious. It is definitely against the monarchy founded on divine
right. It proclaims, to the great horror of the
Journal of Trévoux,[1] the rights of subjects. It
asks that privileges be restricted, that civil
liberty be assured. It desires a constitution.
But it "does not at all approve of the chimera
of absolute equality in a state"; it affirms that,

[1] [The *Journal* (1701-1767), printed at Trévoux (on the
Saône), was the organ of the Jesuits and the arch-foe of the
philosophers.]

if a small state should be republican, "there should be a personal form of government in the larger states."

Even in the case of the ideas which are dearest to them, the philosophers make certain careful distinctions. They believe, for example, that the only instrument of progress is intelligence and that it is an infallible instrument; they should therefore have demanded the diffusion of education. But in the eighteenth century it was the Church which endeavored, and quite successfully, to multiply the primary schools. Neither Voltaire, nor d'Holbach, nor Diderot, nor Louis-Sébastien Mercier, nor Rousseau, nor many others whom we might name demanded equal educational opportunities. They thought that the diffusion of education was practically impossible and dangerous, and the philosopher-procurator, La Chalotais, summed up their opinion of the matter in his *Essay on National Education*: "The welfare of society requires that the knowledge of the people should not extend beyond their daily occupations."

Consequently the philosophers did not at all favor revolution or even thoroughgoing reform but rather the suppression of certain flagrant abuses, so flagrant indeed that no one save those directly interested would defend them. Individual and civil liberty, liberty of conscience, liberty of speech and publication, relative equality in taxation, abolition of such feudal privileges as still existed, liberty of commerce and industry, the reform of the courts, the suppression of bartering in public offices: such is the program of Voltaire, of Diderot, of the *Encyclopedia*, of d'Holbach. That of Mably or Condorcet before the Revolution is not much bolder; it only insists more upon the rights of citizens and upon the necessity of proclaiming these rights. All that might very well have been brought about without any upheaval, and when the actual upheaval came those of the philosophers who survived were at first bewildered, then scandalized. Restif de la Bretonne, L.-S. Mercier, Raynal, Marmontel, even Brissot, do not understand. "The philosophers," concludes Morellet, "neither desired to do all that was actually done, nor to bring it about by the means that were actually adopted, nor to complete it all in as little time as has been found sufficient for the purpose." Not one of his fellow-collaborators of the *Encyclopedia* would have contradicted him. That matters but little, one may say; the revolutionists drew from the works of the encyclopedists the consequences that they themselves had not foreseen but that are necessarily derived from these works. That is merely to give an arbitrary interpretation of the word "necessarily." The opinion of the philosophers was in fact that one could not pass from theory to actual practice without examining, revising, and adapting the theory. One could not really consider oneself a disciple of the philosophers without remaining faithful to this spirit.

PART IV

THE PHILOSOPHY AND THE
LITERATURE OF SENTIMENT

CHAPTER I

PHILOSOPHY

Historical note.—Jean-Jacques Rousseau was born at Geneva in 1712. Badly brought up, apprenticed to a court clerk, then to an engraver, he left Geneva one fine day (1728) to become converted to Catholicism. He was received by a lay missionary of Annecy, Mme de Warens, at whose home he lived, attempting various careers and indulging in sundry escapades, until 1740. One of the happiest periods of his life, so he says, was that spent in a little estate, Les Charmettes, which had been rented by his protectress in the vicinity of Chambéry. But Mme de Warens, who was inconstant, had begun to favor a new protégé, and Jean-Jacques decided to depart for Paris.

There he tried his hand at literature, secured the friendship of Marivaux, Fontenelle, and Diderot, and was named secretary to M. Montaigu, the ambassador at Venice; he left his employ after a quarrel and returned to France in 1744. He then became secretary to Mme Dupin, the wife of a financier. In 1750 he took part in a literary competition of the Academy of Dijon on the subject: "Has the triumph of the arts and sciences contributed to purify morals?" His *Discourse*, which took a negative attitude, won the prize and Rousseau suddenly became famous. Taking part in another literary competition, he composed the *Origin and the Foundations of Inequality among Men* (1754). After a journey to Geneva, in the course of which he returned to Protestantism and reassumed his status as a citizen, he withdrew in

1756 to a little house in the valley of Montmorency, the
Hermitage, which was lent to him by his friend, Mme
d'Épinay. He quarreled with her and took refuge first in
Montmorency, then in an outhouse near the château of
the maréchal de Luxembourg. He published his *Letter to
d'Alembert on Theatrical Performances* (1758), *Émile,
or Of Education* (1762), the *Social Contract* (1762).
The *Émile* was condemned and Rousseau was forced to
flee in order to escape imprisonment. Expelled in turn
from Yverdon in Switzerland, from Motiers near Neuchâtel, from the Ile Saint-Pierre in the lake of Bienne, he
accepted the hospitality offered in England by the philosopher, Hume. But a violent quarrel ensued between the
two, and Rousseau returned to France, where he wandered for some time, a prey to a sort of persecution mania:
finally he returned to Paris (1770). In 1778 he accepted
the hospitality offered him by the marquis de Girardin
on his estate of Ermenonville. There he died in the same
year. The *Confessions*, the dialogues entitled *Rousseau,
Judge of Jean-Jacques*, and the *Reveries of a Solitary
Pedestrian* were published from 1781 to 1790.

Bernardin de Saint-Pierre was born at le Havre in
1737. He served for some time as an army engineer, then
was dismissed and traveled through Holland, Russia,
Poland, and Germany in search of a position, meeting only
with amorous adventures. After a voyage to Mauritius
(1768), he returned to France, where he lived from
hand to mouth. The success of the *Studies of Nature*
brought him both fame and wealth. He later published
Paul and Virginia (1787), the *Indian Hut* (1790), and
a political work, *A Hermit's Vows* (1790). He died in
1814.

The origins of the philosophy of sentiment.
—Even in the seventeenth century philos-

ophy, literature, and life had not always been entirely directed by reason and by luminous ideas. That becomes very evident when we examine the life of the times. If the heroes of Corneille always desire what their reason decides and can always accomplish what they desire, if the heroes of Racine in abandoning themselves to their passions clearly recognize their weakness and the abyss to which it leads them, we know by the memoirs of the century and by hundreds of other documents that in real life the instincts retained their blind power and the passions their confused violence. But the Cartesian philosophy itself encountered certain obstacles at the very outset. It founded philosophy and life upon reason and logic. One could conceive of another philosophy or guide of life; and as a matter of fact the effort was made to establish this dissident philosophy.

This reaction against the sovereignty of reason came from two opposing camps, from religion and from "free thought." Bossuet and Bourdaloue do not doubt that they can give us a clear idea of religion. To believe is to put one's absolute trust in reason; to follow one's religion is to perform an act of conscious wisdom. But after all there was or there might be something quite different in religious faith: enthusiasm, love. One believes in one's God, one gives oneself to Him because one loves Him and not because one has come to realize by dint of reflection that He is the true Deity. This mystic form of piety, this religion of the heart, takes deep root even in the seventeenth century. Religious guidance is not entirely in the hands of those who desire a "reasonable" religion; it is very often entrusted to prominent mystics who care very little about clear and distinct ideas and who deem it sufficient to believe and to teach with fiery ardor and touching pathos. Saint Francis de Sales is perhaps the real spiritual guide of the seventeenth century; and he leads his "Timotheus" along the path of love and ecstasy rather than along that of wisdom and reflection. And yet he is a temperate mystic, who retains even in his most fervid inspiration that moderation in expression that makes him somewhat of a classical literary figure. But there were many other schools of mysticism which cared but little whether they were to be reckoned among the devotees of philosophy or literature and whose leaders are now forgotten; yet these schools conquered the hearts of the multitude. One of them, that of Quietism, is remembered particularly because it aroused a violent dispute among certain illustrious bishops. Whatever the religious value or error of Quietism may be, it provides us with an excellent example of the profound chasm that exists, for men of genius and for their disciples, between the "reason" of the mind and the "reason" of the heart.

Quietism was preached by Mme Guyon. Her particular spiritual adventure would be no more important than other similar adventures of the seventeenth century had it not conquered Fénelon. Clarified by Fénelon, divested of its artlessness and its extravagance of expression, Quietism becomes the religion of "pure love." One believes in one's God and one serves Him not because He is good and just, not because one expects eternal life of Him, but simply because one loves Him; and one would love Him as much even if one were certain of ultimate damnation. A faith of this sort has no need of dogma, of pious practices, of prayers transcribed in words. It is an ecstasy, a communion. If all this be true, intelligence and reflection are not merely useless; they may even become dangerous. One must create for oneself (and this is the very phrase of Fénelon) "the soul of a little child"; one must reduce thought to an instinctive con-

fidence, the inward life to a perpetual sur-
render. Moral progress lies not in the perfection of the mind but in a species of mental
torpor. Mme Guyon was condemned; Fénelon recanted. But other schools of mysticism
appeared at the same time.

The "freethinkers" of the seventeenth century were certainly not mystics, and the pleasures that they sought were by no means "mental prayers"; yet they had a certain ethical
code or at least a certain desire for one. They
knew perfectly that their beloved and indul-
gent "nature" did not supply them with this
code. But in "following the laws of nature"
they could rejoice, as did La Fontaine, in a
fine sky, a good book, a splendid painting, a
sweet reverie, or even a pretty face. These
pleasures were not forbidden; they were even
beneficial beyond any possible doubt. Above
all, the "freethinkers" did not have to reason
or to impose any restraint upon themselves
in order to love their friends dearly, to have
pity for their unfortunate fellow men, to take
pleasure in being helpful, generous, faithful.
This natural moral code was neither mere reasoning nor blind obedience to a rule; it was a
sentiment and might be perfectly valid in
spite of reason. Thus life in its entirety, from

the pleasures of art to those of friendship and
tenderness, can obey forces that intelligence
can hardly justify; yet they are as legitimate
as the rationality of reason itself. This moral
code and "philosophy of the heart" are already
to be found more or less clearly in a Mme
Deshoulières, or a Ninon de Lenclos, or a
Molière, or a La Fontaine. They become more
precise in a Saint-Evremond or a marquis de
Lassay. And toward the end of the seventeenth
century and in the beginning of the eighteenth
there comes into being a sort of romantic system of ethics, which makes the depth of
passion its own justification. To love "madly"
and "desperately" may be an admirable thing
in spite of the element of moral delinquency
involved and in spite of human and divine
laws, if love represents the utter abandonment
of self and the ardor of sacrifice. One reads
and rereads two works that afford admirable
examples of such a love as this: the *Letters of
Héloïse and Abelard* and the *Letters of a
Portuguese Nun*. The *Portuguese Letters* pass
through at least ten editions; there are more
than fifty editions, adaptations, or interpretations of the *Letters of Héloïse*.

The "forces of sentiment" also intervene in
literary discussions and doctrines. They are

purposely ignored in the classical period, or at
most only fleeting allusions are made to them.
Fénelon believes in these forces even if he does
not theorize about them. When, in the *Letter
to the Academy*, he must choose between the
ancients and the moderns, he gives hardly any
arguments in favor of the ancients; he contents
himself with saying: "I love the ancient classics"; and then he cites them for the purpose of
being able to say to us: "You see that I am right
in loving them as I do." This "sentimental
criticism" is not immediately successful; it is
not upheld by those who are dominating literary opinion at the time, by Fontenelle and
La Motte. But it rapidly imposes itself. It is
really the type of criticism that Marivaux
defends when wittily but with profound conviction he postulates the theory of the "I don't
know what" as a basis of literary criticism.
For the elegant phrases of Marivaux, the
Reflections on Poetry and Painting by the
abbé Dubos (1719) substitute able and sound
reasoning: "The method of discussion is not as
valid in ascertaining the merit of a poem or of
a painting as is that of sentiment." And sentiment is not the business of professional critics
and pedants. Their "sensibility" is frayed,
their hearts are "perfectly calloused."

Jean-Jacques Rousseau.—It is clear that J.-J. Rousseau did not entirely invent the philosophy of sentiment. When he speaks of taste and of criticism he does not add very much to what he has read in Dubos, Levesque de Pouilly, Father André. However, it was Rousseau who made sentiment not a mere chapter or aspect of philosophy but a new philosophy, set up against rationalistic philosophy. It was he who made the doctrine famous. Neither Voltaire, nor Helvétius, nor Diderot, nor Condorcet can give a detailed and individual account of the rationalistic or realistic philosophy, whereas Rousseau is quite able to sum up, and in brilliant fashion, the philosophy of sentiment.

He does not come upon it at the very outset. When he leaves Les Charmettes and comes to Paris, he has an idea of advancing his career exactly as the rest have done, by becoming a fashionable wit and a philosopher. He becomes intimate with philosophers, with Mably, Condillac, Diderot; he admires Voltaire. He visits "philosophical" *salons* like those of Mme Dupin, Mme d'Épinay, M. de la Popelinière. His convictions or his indifference, his morals or his immorality are philosophical. He is one of the collaborators of the *Encyclopedia*. Even when he writes the *Discourse on the Sciences and the Arts* or that *On the Origin of Inequality among Men*, he does not at all realize that he is abandoning the philosophers. He does not have that impression when he writes the first of these discourses, nor is it particularly strong even when he writes the second. In discussing the progress of intelligence or the idea of property he reasons exactly as a philosopher might reason, basing his argumentation upon logic, historical facts, natural history, travels. His conclusions even interest philosophers without necessarily scandalizing them. For a long time men had been reflecting upon the savages and had been considering them to be happy. For a long time they had been discussing rationally the benefits or the misdeeds of the stage, of novels, of luxury, or even of academies. Rousseau was more eloquent, more decisive than the others; but others, including even the *Encyclopedia* at times, had often arrived at the same conclusions as he.

What was originally an intellectual enthusiasm gradually became for Rousseau a profound conviction, a necessity, a guide of life. He was not a very successful wit because he was not versed (or so he thought, at any rate) in the art of entertaining; he was not a real philosopher because he found no genuine pleasure in analyzing ideas and constructing systems. The exercise of reason was for him a laborious and not an agreeable activity. Besides, he thought that this activity was not only useless but dangerous. To be sure, he had acquired considerable reputation because of his reasoning ability; but he was neither happier nor better for that. In fact he was not a good man: he had sent his children to the Foundlings' Home; and he was not happy. All the occupations of his mind left his heart empty. He came to the conclusion that his mode of living should be governed not by his reason but by his heart.

He resolved therefore to live according to the dictates of his heart. He renounced society, every appearance of luxury, even the fellowship of the philosophers, and almost all books. He shut himself up in the solitude of the Hermitage, in that of Montlouis, and later that of Montmorency. He began to dream, not to reason, to contemplate, not to discuss, to "let his heart and not his mind express itself." To the reality of his solitary and rustic life, to the murmur of April brooks, to the freshness of periwinkles, to the perfume of the orange blossoms of the château of Montmorency, he wished to add his "golden age," his "empyrean"; he constructed out of the fabric of reverie a world in which happiness and wisdom had nothing in common with the happiness and wisdom of the worldly wise. The real sages, "ignorant of philosophy" and disdainful of reason, are encouraged by a certitude that is at the same time more consoling and more unconditioned; they are persons like Julie and Saint-Preux in the *Modern Héloïse* or the tutor and the vicar of Savoy in *Émile*.

Certainly they do not imagine themselves exempt from the possibility of error. Their hearts urge them on; they are guilty according to worldly standards, or one may even say that they are guilty, without qualification of any sort. Julie becomes the mistress of Saint-Preux; and the vicar has had his moments of weakness. But the reason of the philosophers is not a better guide than sentiment. It has nothing but excuses to offer for faults that are far graver than those of Julie and Saint-Preux; it is amused at adultery even when it does not justify it. And it has nothing but cynical irony and desperate negation to offer to those who are seeking a guide to life. Of course, it is true that one may live decently

even if one is a skeptic and a philosopher:
Rousseau thinks so or tries to think so for a
few months after the publication of the *Modern
Héloïse*. M. de Wolmar, Julie's husband, possesses all the human virtues and he makes
Julie happy; yet he does not believe in God.
But Rousseau is very quickly persuaded that
virtue of that type is either a deceitful affec-
tation or else tends inevitably to adopt those
sentiments that the philosophers deny. The
skepticism of M. de Wolmar is overwhelmed
by despair at the death of his loved one. He
must either succumb to the horror of it all or
else seek renunciation. Consequently, at the
end of the novel M. de Wolmar is on the
threshold of conversion. He returns to religion, or rather to the religious philosophy
of Julie and Saint-Preux.

Julie and Saint-Preux present this philosophy in the course of their romance of love
and resignation. The vicar of Savoy demonstrates it more methodically and at great
length. The reasoning of philosophy—and not
only that of books but that of drinking bouts
and worldly conversation—explains the soul
by the various properties of the body, of the
brain, of the nerves. The body itself is only one
form of living matter; and living matter is

only one of the aspects of matter, the only reality of the universe. This conclusion destroys the soul, liberty, virtue, that is to say, every reason for living. Happily, it is easy to demonstrate that these conclusions are paradoxes and that this "logic" is a succession of illogical arguments. One may take the trouble, as Rousseau did in the *Profession of Faith of the Vicar of Savoy*, to demonstrate all that; but it is quite useless to do so. If we are sincere with ourselves, if we are not blinded by partisan spirit, we must feel that even if the arguments of the philosophers were impeccable, they could not convince us. "A voice rises within us," a voice that nothing can silence, the teachings of which are clear, imperious, decisive. It is conscience, "divine instinct." By virtue of my conscience I *feel*—and nothing can prevail against this sentiment—that I am free to do good or evil, that my immortal soul will be rewarded for the good, and punished for the evil that I may do, by a God who is compassionate and paternal.

Here are the truths that suffice. Rousseau indeed has presented all this not merely as an exhortation but as a real philosophy. And this philosophy applies methods that have nothing in common with those of the the so-called "philosophers." The truths postulated by Julie, by Wolmar, or by the vicar of Savoy are true because they have the necessary support of sentiment, just as the axioms of geometry or the "I think, therefore I exist" of Descartes have for them the necessary support of reason. But they are true, furthermore, because they are efficacious; in fact they are the only efficacious truths. How could practical philosophy affect the lives of Saint-Preux, Julie, M. de Wolmar, Émile? M. de Wolmar realizes that he practises justice and goodness in spite of his doctrines, or at least quite ignoring them. If Julie and Saint-Preux followed the philosophical maxims, they would be adulterous. Without doubt, they could not demonstrate by geometrical theorems that they are right in not being adulterous and in preferring redemption to perseverance in sin, heroic responsibility to sated desire. But they *feel* that it is their unproved principles of life that give their manner of living its validity. Like the philosopher who proves movement by walking, they demonstrate their moral certitude by the dignity and the beneficence of their lives. One must judge the tree by its fruits. The philosophical fruits are bitter and poisonous; they are pernicious, they are false.

The fruits of "conscience" and of "sentiment" are vivifying; they are true.

The influence of the doctrine.—This was not merely a new doctrine, a sort of "pragmatism"; it was a battle cry. Rousseau did not content himself with refuting theories, with opposing discussion by discussion. He attacked men; he doomed them to scorn. For a long time he had been considered as one of the group of the Encyclopedists, the pernicious philosophers, the "Cacouacs," as they are called in the satire by Moreau. The comedy of the *Philosophers* of Palissot caricatured him as maliciously as it did Diderot or Helvétius. But now Rousseau left the philosophical camp. He isolated himself in the woods; one no longer saw him in the *salons*. Then he quarreled violently with Voltaire, Diderot, Grimm, Mme d'Épinay, d'Holbach; the *Émile* brought about the definite break. In the *Modern Héloïse* the philosopher as exemplified in the person of M. de Wolmar is inconsequent, indeed, but quite sympathetic, while the *Profession of Faith of the Vicar of Savoy* expressly demonstrates that the philosophers are the enemies of the human race. All this did not make Jean-Jacques a defender of the Church and an avenger of tradition. The authorities were aroused to adopt sterner measures toward him than toward men like Voltaire or Helvétius. Rousseau, expelled from France, expelled from Geneva, from Yverdon, from Motiers, from the Ile Saint-Pierre, was forced to the wandering life of the exile. Yet, although the fact was not definitely suspected at the time, this philosophy of sentiment was about to renew religious philosophy and to create a philosophy of its own.

In their warfare upon "libertines" and philosophers, the defenders of the Church had availed themselves of philosophical methods. To demonstrations they opposed other demonstrations; to logical arguments, other logical arguments. They sought a weapon in real reason as against false reason. But the reason of the philosophers had in its favor novelty, clarity (at least apparent clarity), talent. The defenders of tradition were not endowed with talent; they persisted in their academic argumentation, in a scholasticism or a logic compounded with scholasticism, from which contemporary minds inevitably turned away. Arguments like the insults of the *Journal of Trévoux* or of Lefranc de Pompignan caused mere boredom or ridicule. To escape it, the defenders of Catholicism attempted a new

method which failed, and adopted another
which succeeded.

The one that failed was the Voltairian
method. It was decided to conquer wit by wit
and to oppose irony with irony. The lawyer,
Moreau, writes the *Outline of the History of
the Cacouacs*, the abbé Barruel, the *Helvien-
nes or Philosophical Provincial Letters*
(1781), the abbé Feller a *Philosophical Catechism* (1773) ; in these works the stupidity and
the folly of philosophers are lampooned.
These jests are of no avail: one must have
something besides sincerity to match the wit
of a Voltaire or the vivacity of a Diderot.
But sincerity and genuine emotion suffice to
move, or at least not to bore. Rousseau in
"appealing to the heart" reveals to those who
wish to write of faith and piety that instead
of seeking to *demonstrate* it may be sufficient
for their purpose to *move*. Of course one cannot thus establish strictly Catholic or even
Christian philosophy. The "delights and beau-
ties" of religion are not the precise formulas
of the dogmas and the commandments; and
the religion of the heart was preached by all
sorts of disciples who were only deists and not
Christians. But at least these deists and Christians no longer opposed each other; they

sought communion in the same contemplations and the same effusions. "Natural religion" was no longer a sort of philosophical condescension, an argumentative abstraction. It became an impulse of the heart, a sentiment of love and of the divine presence; and in this sentiment believers, doubters, and non-believers might unite or at least no longer combat one another. Philosophy had set up against religion the formula "All or nothing"; if you do not believe that religion is true in every particular, you are against it, you are on the side of the philosophers. On the contrary, Rousseau creates an intermediary type between strict orthodoxy and philosophical negation: that is, religiosity. And religiosity is the road by which one often returns to religion.

It would be a lengthy task to enumerate the works in which the hearts of men "rise to God," in which the author meditates on "the goodness of God," in which "conscience reveals His holy name." It would be necessary to quote priests' sermons, odes and elegies, pious pamphlets and manuals, moral tales and romances, the testimony of memoirs, journals, correspondence. One would have to mention the officer, Séguier de Saint-Brisson, the poet, Léonard, the novelists, La Dixmerie,

Durosoy, Sabatier de Castres and Mme Le-
prince de Beaumont, the minister, Necker, the
abbé Gérard, and the *Comte de Valmont, or
the Errors of Reason*, which was the most
widely read defense of Christianity toward the
close of the eighteenth century. It will be sufficient for our purpose to confine ourselves to
Bernardin de Saint-Pierre, whose work sums
up excellently that of all the rest.

At first he indulges in a bit of nonsense.
Rousseau would have had religion consist of
murmuring: "Oh, great Being! Oh, great
Being!" and of going into raptures at the
goodness of Providence. Bernardin de Saint-
Pierre (and a few others) carried ecstasy to
certain extremes which have become famous.
Providence has given ample testimony of its
beneficence, according to him, by providing
the melon with ribs so that it may more easily
be eaten in a family group. His *Studies of
Nature* are not scientific according to the
standards of geometricians and philosophers.
But Bernardin de Saint-Pierre disdains this
science; it is mendacious and it is harmful:
and it is mendacious because it is harmful.
He gives the clearest and bluntest formula of
this "pragmatism": "First of all one must seek
truth with one's heart, not with one's mind.

The mind has no science that the heart cannot comprehend. Science has led us by delightful routes to a rather frightful goal. Its ambitious researches drag in their train that ancient malediction pronounced against the first who dared to eat of the fruit of the tree." The *Studies* and their formulas were most brilliantly successful. Bernardin de Saint-Pierre awoke one day to find himself famous. His demonstrations were "harmonies," physical and moral "harmonies," "charms" and "delights," melancholies and reveries, brilliantly colored tableaux and pathetic tableaux. Certainly *Paul and Virginia*, which was a later production, did not *prove* that harmony, devotion, tenderness are born in hearts that are not misled by the lies of the cities. The religion and the morals of Paul and Virginia are not demonstrated but merely described. But after all it was precisely description and not demonstration that was desired. Of what importance were the arguments of Voltaire, the criticisms of the Bible, and the misdeeds of fanaticism when one was touched, carried away, convinced? One wept and one believed when one read one's prayers at the water's edge: "I saw a group of young peasant girls, fair as are most of the maidens of Caux; they

were leaving the village, their long white
headdresses fluttering about their faces. . . .
One of them kept aloof, sad and pensive. . . .
She approached a large shrine in the middle
of the pier, drew some money from her pocket,
put it in the box which was at the base of the
shrine; then she knelt and said her prayers,
her hands clasped and her eyes raised to
heaven. The waves which were deafening as
they cast themselves upon the shore, the wind
which shook the great lanterns of the crucifix,
the danger threatening upon the sea, and the
peasant girl's trust in God gave to her love a
grandeur and a majesty that the great could
never know in their mighty palaces!"

CHAPTER II

LITERATURE AND THE MORAL CODE OF SENTIMENT

Rousseau and the delights of sentiment.—
Of course Rousseau's philosophy had a moral
code as its consequence. Conscience does not
merely reveal to us with rigorous certainty
God, Providence, and the immortality of the
soul. It enables us to know by the same decisive intuition what is good and what is bad,
not the complicated exigencies of the social
moral code, which are often useless or immoral, but at any rate the simple laws of conduct that teach us to be upright, sincere, compassionate, helpful. For those who were not
interested by, or rather shocked at, the abundant discourse of the vicar of Savoy, the
demonstration, or rather the presentation, of
this intuitive and beneficent moral code was
given at length in the *Modern Héloïse*. Even
if they do not speak of prayer, of Providence,
or of morality, Julie and Saint-Preux offer us

rules for the conduct of life. The account of their lives is not meant merely to move us; Rousseau wishes it to be taken as a model. Philosophy, morality, literature are therefore closely linked in his thoughts. But although there was a widely prevalent belief, in the eighteenth century, in the moral code of Rousseau or in an analogous moral code, this belief did not imply acceptance of his general philosophy. One taught and practised this moral code without concerning oneself in the slightest about principles or philosophy. . . . Taken all in all, it was a literary and practical moral code that was created, rather than a systematic one.

The principle of this code is that one does not reason about morality; one feels it: it is not governed by mind but by emotion. And our will to obey this code comes not from reflective will power, from a calculated effort, but from an instinctive impulse, from a necessity of the heart. Even to do good by the exercise of will power, to follow moral teachings through obedience, is to subject oneself to a painful discipline; it is to make an effort and to suffer. But it is not necessary that moral precepts should involve sacrifice. Even in the most extreme cases these precepts would require less painful sacrifice than any others. Saint-Preux and Julie suffer greatly when they must abandon their love; but they would suffer even more if they were to drive the parents of Julie to despair. Very often, even, the accomplishment of one's duty becomes a profound source of joy rather than a sacrifice; one sacrifices oneself because one loves; one is generous because one's heart is moved. And in the emotions of love and generosity there is ample reward for one's sacrifice. This conception of morality and of virtue is not altogether original. It is to be found earlier in the *Morals* of Toussaint: "Love alone can make us faithful to our duties." It is implied in the "tearful comedy" of Nivelle de la Chaussée. His heroes are right when they move us; we approve of them when our hearts make us their accomplices. Finally we have much the same idea in other novels, long before the *Modern Héloïse*. However, such cases as the above are not general before 1760; it is Rousseau who gives to morality based on sentiment the form that tends to triumph in the eighteenth century.

Before Rousseau certain concessions had already been made to sentiment. It was no longer a principle of error or of weakness;

it was one of the legitimate forces of life. But
it was not the essential element of life, or at
least it was not its only guide. When it invaded
the entire soul and dominated one's whole destiny, it was an accident which became the
subject of a novel or a play; it was not an ideal.
For Rousseau, however, the only "active"
principle in the soul is sentiment; the value of
one's life is to be measured in terms of the
rôle that sentiment plays therein. And the
more ardent it is, the more certain it is; the
more exclusive it is, the more enviable it is.
M. de Wolmar has all the satisfactions of rational "wisdom"; he does whatever he desires,
and all that he desires is just and sensible. All
that, however, avails nothing when he first
knows Julie. Sentiment, no matter how re-
strained and unimpassioned it may be, is
superior to all one's philosophic past, to
all the joys of reason. Saint-Preux might
very well be a philosopher; he can read, observe, and discuss as well as anyone else.
But all philosophies and even all practical
activities seem to him to be vain. He traverses
the *salons* of Paris; he is initiated into politics
by an English peer; he makes a journey
around the world. But it is all to no purpose.
Neither the delights of science nor those of

travel are worth a single moment of his happiness with Julie or a single hour of his love torments. He will again feel a desire to live, he will again interest himself in his destiny, and in destiny in general, only when he will love again and will give freely of devotion. He will enjoy the rustic domesticity of the château of Wolmar because there nobody lives for his own pleasure, for ambition, for material gain, but for the pleasure and the prosperity of others. Consequently the entire mode of living of the century must be changed. One must neither say: "Live in order to learn and to understand," nor "Live in order to obey order and rules"; but "Live in order to love your fellow beings, in order to bind yourself to them, in order to hearken to the voice of your heart. In doing so you will be doing what is righteous, and you will have nothing more to learn."

The fatal gift of heaven.—One can easily see the consequences of this doctrine; they have been abundantly denounced since the time of Rousseau and especially since the Romantic period. Rousseau himself was impelled to admit in writing his *Letters*, his *Reveries*, and his *Confessions* that there were in the heart and in sentiment certain obscure recesses and certain mysterious forces that might well foster a sentiment quite distinct from peace, enthusiasm, or ecstasy. He felt in himself an "inexplicable ill," a "void that could not be filled." Saint-Preux, thinking of his brief period of felicity and his prolonged torments, denounced the "fatal gift of heaven." In a word, he perceived that the faculty of feeling was the faculty of suffering. And the suffering of sensitive souls might easily lead them to uneasiness, confusion, the *tædium vitæ*. All these ideas had already appeared in literature before Rousseau. Here and there tormented souls or novelists had depicted the bittersweet of ardent passion. One "drinks deep of its poison." Anticipating the very phraseology of Rousseau, one tastes its "fatal sweetness," the "griefs that can delight," "delightful sadness," and even "the fatal gift of heaven." But neither the *Letters of a Portuguese Nun*, nor Baculard d'Arnaud, nor the chevalier de Mouhy, nor any of the others had really conquered public opinion. Rousseau, however, had straightway subjugated it with his *Modern Héloïse*.

The *Héloïse* was eagerly sought and purchased; one spent one's night reading it. It was lent at the rate of ten *sous* an hour per

volume. In the most distant provinces, at Vrés
or at Hennebont, it was awaited feverishly;
there was general disappointment at receiving
only spurious copies. And in the *Héloïse* one
eagerly sought not only the advice that Rousseau gave openly but also that which he merely
suggested. Men as well as women have their
fill of anguish and tears, and intoxicate themselves with the "delights of sentiment." The
future general, the baron Thiébault, cannot
finish his reading of the work without shout-
ing, without "howling like a wild beast." And
one is persuaded by what is henceforth to be
taught by the heroes and heroines of twenty
other novels. "Sensibility" is a "divine inspiration." "Oh, sensibility," sighs one of these
heroes, "it is with thee that I would live,
whether happy or unhappy!" Love itself is no
longer sufficient for such as these. They must
plunge themselves in ecstasy, and blend extreme felicity with the horrors of an obscure
anguish: "To enjoy such felicity and to sur-
vive it. . . . Is that sensibility?" "O God,
with what manner of soul hast Thou endowed
me? My love terrifies me and I should despair if I were to be deprived of it!" These
despairing creatures who cultivate their misery and drape their lives in funeral veils are

multiplied by novelists before *Werther*, thirty years before *Obermann* and *René*.

It is not Rousseau, however, who is responsible, or if so, his responsibility is very slight. Romantic pessimism is only suggested in what his contemporaries read, in the *Héloïse*. They did not know the *Reveries* and the *Confessions* until the eighties. Long before these two works, illustrious or merely prolix works had lavished sepulchral settings, had sung of the somber fascination of death and had diligently lamented the sad destiny of humanity. The heroes of the abbé Prévost, Cleveland, and Patrick in the *Dean of Killerine*, traverse life bending under the weight of an obscure fatality. Unfortunately they aggravate their sufferings by their intensive introspection; even when they are fortunate, they poison their happiness by foreboding of the morrow. After 1750 and especially after 1760 "somber" literature and "sinister" literature no longer represent a mere tendency but a passion, and a very ardent one. Translations are made of the *Meditations* of Hervey (1770) and the *Elegy Composed in a Country Churchyard* of Gray (1768). Feutry publishes his *Temple of Death* in 1753 and his *Tombs*. One of the books that is most widely read,

commented upon, and imitated is the translation of the *Nights* (1769), in which the
English poet, Young, tells how he buried his
daughter by the tragic light of a lantern, medi-
tating all the while upon the vanity of life.
Then the "somber" element invades literature,
but no effort is made to justify that literary
type by an appeal to Rousseau's example or
to his work. Baculard d'Arnaud uses pro-
fusely the element of the "somber" in the
Recreations of the Sentimental and the *Ordeals of Sentiment*. He boasts of having
invented the "somber" drama; and the invention was successful. In 1776 a translation is
made of the *Werther* of Goethe; and before
1797 there are fifteen translations, adaptations,
or new editions of the work. Léonard and
Loaisel de Tréogate even begin to make their
novels the passionate avowal of the torments
of their own hearts. The writer, in order to
intensify his sufferings, offers himself as a prey
to the curiosity of his readers. All the specifically Romantic ills enter the tale and the
novel.

The delights of virtue.—But these ills constituted only a passing error and an accident
without serious consequences for Rousseau,
his disciples, and the rest. They believed in

the "charms of sensibility" and in the "delights of the heart" because they were firmly persuaded that these were also the charms and the delights of virtue. For these early Romanticists sensibility and passion were virtues, in fact the only virtues. Above the vulgar moral precepts and prejudices, passion, a divine inspiration, establishes its laws. It is one with duty. And when it conflicts with certain duties that contradict it, it is these duties that are at fault. But there was never any contradiction of that type in the case of our Romanticists of the eighteenth century. They all accepted the certainties postulated by Rousseau, whether or not they were his disciples. Now in the *Modern Héloïse*, which in the eighteenth century was a sort of Bible of sentiment, whenever passion conflicts with the old morality, with that of all societies since the epoch of the Bible, it is passion that yields or that makes an effort to yield. Saint-Preux and Julie might be happy in marriage; Julie has merely to abandon her tyrannical father. After her marriage to de Wolmar, Saint-Preux and she might attempt another sort of happiness, that adultery which in the aristocratic society of the century is the great compromise between the marriage forced upon young ladies and the right of "following the dictates of one's own heart." But in order that Julie may remain faithful to her filial duties, Saint-Preux leaves her, and they both resign themselves to her marriage with M. de Wolmar, who is fifty years old and whom she does not love. Instead of returning to Julie after she is married, Saint-Preux leaves for his voyage around the world. And when he returns to the château of Wolmar, it is to admire the mode of life of its inhabitants; this mode of life is inspired by virtues and by ideals which are anything but romantic. For the dwellers at the château live not for exaltation but for tranquil peace or resignation, not for adventure but for obscure toil, not to rise up in revolt against the universe but to seek self-forgetfulness in devoting oneself to others. The *Modern Héloïse* is at the same time the hymn of sensibility and the poem of middle-class virtues.

Now the public in general found as much pleasure in the poem as in the hymn. The best proof of that is that readers generally did not observe the possibly disturbing elements in the morality of the *Héloïse*; for it must be confessed that if Julie dies virtuous, her virtue is sorely beset toward the end. Philosophers like Voltaire, Marmontel, La Harpe,

and Mme Necker, as well as critics who were
offended by the religion of Julie, did not hesitate to denounce the "poison" and the "sophist-
ry" of the novel. But these were either philosophers or else people whose manifest duty
it was to defend the orthodox religion. All the
others, even the most prudent and the most
staid, drew from the novel—or thought so at
any rate—only lessons of virtue and abnegation; and these included the *Mercury of
France* as well as the *Literary Year*, the competitors of the Floral Games as well as Protestant pastors, women as well as men, humble
folk as well as wealthy folk. All are of the
opinion of Manon Phlipon, the future Mme
Roland, that one must "have a sordid soul
indeed" not to feel the virtuous power of the
novel; or as Mme de Staël puts it, "married
people should read the *Héloïse*. They will feel
more inspired with love for virtue."

The novelists too, whether or not they ac-
knowledge Rousseau as their master, associate
sentiment with virtue and as often as not the
heroism of virtue with the exaltation of sentiment. They distinguish—and that is one of the
aspects of Romanticism—between the virtues
established by "prejudice" and the real virtues. And when one knows the prejudices that

they condemn, it is difficult not to agree heartily
with these novelists. Their revolt against the
existing social order is limited to a protest
against the obligation laid upon a girl to marry
the rich old man or the influential rustic whom
her father favors, or against the social scorn
for the girl who has been seduced. For the
rest, our novelists require of sentiment that it
inspire abnegation, fidelity, modesty. All their
heroes resemble those of Corneille: they triumph over the most vehement passions. Only
it is not because their reason reigns triumphant
over their passions; it is because they yield to
the impulses of their hearts, which are more
desirous of virtuous suffering than of guilty
happiness. They combine "all the ecstasy of
passion with all the dignity of virtue." A
"secret enthusiasm" uplifts them. Their hearts
are "warmed by sentiment only to be exalted
by virtue." And there reappears the doctrine
of the beneficent passions that is becoming
continually more explicit. "There can be no
virtue without passions; only passions constitute the virtuous man." "Oh, religion!
Oh, sacred duties! Oh, virtues of sensibility!" Through "sensibility" we become
"demi-gods." For God is the "very God of
sensibility"; the soul ravished unto the very

heavens seems to merge there with that divinity from which it receives the germ of precious love, the life of the universe, the source of all happiness, an eternal flame bestowing upon virtue that heroic warmth which is so necessary for its very existence."

The general literary movement.—It is, of course, in the novels of the century that what is already called the "flood of sensibility" courses most impetuously. Rousseau dominates the novel and it is his name that we have especially encountered up to the present time. But the torrent of sensibility has more than one source. It does not come from the *Héloïse* alone; it is augmented by many other streams.

First there is the drama, upon which Rousseau has no influence; this includes the "tearful comedy" of Nivelle de la Chaussée, the *Cénie* of Mme de Graffigny and certain other plays: the English dramas of Lillo and Moore, the *Gambler* (translated in 1762) and the *Merchant of London* (translated in 1748). Finally Diderot's influence was also very great. This drama of the eighteenth century presents all sorts of novelties which have nothing to do with sensibility; there is an attempt to depict social conditions and not merely characters and customs; there is a desire to introduce "pantomime" and "tableaux," that is to say, eloquence of attitude and gesture and not mere discourse. There is often introduced the element of the "somber" or the "sinister," that is to say, the "terror" of the Crébillon school, supplemented by "convulsions" and other horrors hitherto unimagined. But after all, the leading note of this drama is sensibility: the dramatic presentation of those emotions that represent neither the smile of comedy nor the anguish of tragedy. The situations merely have to be "touching" (that is, their heroes must be worthy, amiable, and unhappy) to be considered true to life and replete with dramatic force. A beautiful, diligent, and virtuous seamstress is loved by a young nobleman who cannot marry her without driving his family to despair. A young workingman who is intelligent, diligent, and respectable loves the daughter of a rich merchant who rejects the young man's suit. A young peasant who is a soldier, virtuous, and affianced finds himself a deserter against his will; he is about to be shot when his betrothed, a peasant girl who is beautiful and virtuous, wins his pardon. These are the subjects "that make sweet tears flow," that are the delight of "sentimental souls,"

that is to say, of almost everybody. And when
one wishes to parody the drama of the time,
one entitles one's parody the *Scavenger* so that
it may represent the description of a plebeian
social stratum, but one likewise calls it the
Sentimental Scavenger because there is no
drama without sensibility.

Sensibility it is that adds charm to the
moral tale and the "descriptive poem," not to
mention the idyl and the elegy. The moral
tale is invented toward 1760 by a philosopher,
Marmontel; in it he introduces in abundant
measure what he considers to be philosophy:
justice, tolerance, natural religion. But when
he realizes the success of this literary type he
lavishes in an ever-increasing degree tender
hearts, good fathers, virtuous maidens, heroic
fiancés, faithful lovers, constant spouses. Morality therein is a morality of innocence, of
compassion, of worthy effusions. Numerous
imitators follow his example, adding lyricism,
metaphors, and exclamation points; they teach
that one loves virtue as one loves one's dog,
one's turtledove, or one's mother, that is, in
order to feel certain "palpitations of the
heart." And it is precisely this type of morality that is to pervade the "descriptive poem."
This poetic type represents the attempt made

in the second half of the eighteenth century
to rediscover poetical inspiration. Saint-Lambert and the others understand (at least until
1789) that one cannot describe for the sake of
describing, that if poetry could, and in fact
should, be a "painting," it is not supposed to
paint merely any chance object: it should deal
with that which is more or less universal. It
should be, if one may say so, a "painting" of
sensibility. Saint-Lambert is a very dry
philosopher, Delille is an educator who is
very skillful in furthering his own interests;
but both follow the fashion, as does Roucher,
who is really poetically gifted. And it is the
fashion to be moved and to shed gentle tears
over plowmen, over village betrothals, over
rose-queens, and benevolent squires, over the
pure joys of rustic life, over romantic gardens
and landscapes, over melancholy groves and
the altars of reverie. Poetry is born of the sorrow, the "sweet effusions," even the "tempests," of the heart. The descriptive poets
really understand one of the characteristics of
poetry. All that they lack is sincerity and
talent.

They understand this particular characteristic of poetry well and they follow the right
path in seeking it. They do not find it in Louis

Racine or in J.-B. Rousseau or in the *Henriade*; but they read the English poets. "Anglomania" represents not merely the mania for English breakfasts, English liberty, English philosophy and horse-racing. It manifests itself also in delight in Gray, Hervey, Shakespeare, and Ossian. Of course, as we have previously noted, even when one is "entirely English" one is in reality a very good Frenchman. All the translations from the English correct and adapt the original, and many utterly disguise it. The Shakespeare of Ducis is a caricature and that of Letourneur, a travesty. The *Ossian* of this same Letourneur has been sent to the school of "taste" and "propriety." But nevertheless Shakespeare is admired because he represents "the great crises of the soul," because he inspires "confused and profound emotion," because he "raises man above himself." Ossian in particular was a revelation. In spite of the timidity or the awkwardness of the translations, he was a sort of conjurer of the mist, a master of reverie. He revealed strong, impulsive, and passionate heroes, settings that were filled with the "soul of solitude" and the "phantoms of the imagination," the silent moors, the haunted heaths of mists and of specters, the glaucous and sonorous ocean. He substituted for mythological marvels, which were academic and lifeless, the romantic and genuine marvels of legend.

Moreover, a definite theory of this "poetry of the heart" and of "enthusiasm" is postulated; or rather, it is eloquently affirmed that real poetry is superior to all rules and theories. Over the ruins of the old "poetic arts" the "poet of genius" goes whithersoever his genius may lead him, quite unfettered. The very philosophers support this viewpoint in spite of their confidence in reason. "No sooner has the learned pedant established his poetical system on supposedly invariable principles, no sooner has he revealed all the sources of the Beautiful and uttered a malediction upon those who would seek it elsewhere, than a man of genius appears, violates every tenet that the critic has established, and produces an immortal work." Grimm is rather pedantic in thus assailing pedantry. But his friend, Diderot, in turn creates an exalted, one might almost say giddily exalted, image of the poet and the man of genius. It is upon the mountain tops, in the sacred horror of the forests, in the mouth of somber caverns, hard by the tumult of wild torrents that a certain Dorval, who is represented as being a typical "poet of

genius," seeks inspiration. He must have the
wind disheveling his locks, he must hear the
great voices of solitude, he must seek communion with the mysteries of things and the
immensity of space. Great poetry can be born
only of an immense crisis, a crisis not merely
in one soul but in all souls. It is necessary that
some tremendous social shock, by disrupting
order, equilibrium, and tradition, should
cause humanity to indulge again in those
fierce and moving instincts which only poetry
can translate and which alone can create poetry.

Many poets, critics, even pedants and college teachers express the same idea as Diderot,
though less lyrically. "Genius that is enlightened by profound sagacity judges usage before
submitting to it. . . . Rules, precepts, custom, nothing can impede it; nothing can
slacken the rapidity of its course; from its
very first soaring it wings its way to the sublime." The man of genius is a lofty soul,
like a "cliff the height and the steepness of
which terrify us; its crest, towering up,
seems to be suspended aloft. . . . Its aspect
produces a vivid impression of fear." It is not
Rousseau who speaks thus nor even a "sentimental soul"; it is a writer of treatises, it is

Séran de la Tour in his *Art of Feeling and Judging in Matters of Taste* (1762). Men like Louis-Sébastien Mercier or Dorat-Cubières, who pride themselves on being above "wretched prejudice" and "fatal convention," speak with more directness. "Happy is that primitive people that modifies at will its ideas, its sentiments and its pleasures! Unhampered in its service of nature, it gives itself up to the effect and does not reason about the cause. It rejoices, it weeps, it admires; and its rejoicing, its weeping, and its admiration are not conditioned by reasoning examination or the dictates of taste." For the only art that is henceforth recognized is that which rises from the heart; and the only "rule" of this art is sensibility.

Chapter III

SOCIAL IDEAS AND LIFE

We have seen that sentiment was becoming the principle, or at least one of the principles, of philosophy and art. It was inevitable that it should also become the principle of life itself in its social and personal aspects.

It was generally agreed, to begin with, that society should not be founded upon force. Nor was pure reason able to organize and control life; the conviction had grown that the lessons of observation and experience were also requisite. But observation and experience revealed that no society is possible without some sort of mystical belief. Men do not obey the laws and respect the social order merely because they are afraid of the gendarme or the tyrant who dominates them. For the most part, they continue to believe that their obedience is inherent in the very nature of things, that it is in conformity with a superior and recondite will. In despotic society, or one may even say in any form of society, it is religion that defines and delimits this will: such had been the belief up to this time. Now that religion was being suppressed or transformed, the necessity was felt of replacing it by some other form of discipline; this new discipline was to be the "social moral code."

There is no social moral code in the seventeenth century; it is believed that morality is a personal affair and that it can only interest each one of us individually. Each one is responsible for his own moral progress or backslidings; each one is responsible for his own salvation and nobody else's. Charity itself is not given, like that of Don Juan, for "the love of humanity" but for the love of God; it has not as its chief end the happiness of somebody else but one's own spiritual perfection. Nor is there any marked code of civic morality in the seventeenth century. One does not devote oneself to one's nation or fatherland but to one's prince. The principle of the monarchy, as Montesquieu has remarked, is honor. And honor is an exchange of recompense for devotion between the sovereign and those of his subjects who serve him and whose ancestors served his ancestors. The rest of the nation has only the duty of obedience. But in the eighteenth century the philosophers no longer understand charity and they are not interested in unrequited honor; the "sentimental souls" are no longer pious souls and are not aristocratic souls; the social moral code therefore replaces charity and honor.

Its first precept is that it is impossible to maintain a political system or even the social order itself if the State does not take it upon itself to teach and, so to speak, to "organize" the moral code. In the past it relied upon deceitful religions and avaricious priests; henceforth the State will direct these priests and will determine what they are to teach. Rousseau, in the *Social Contract*, foresees a religion of the State which is to be selected before the conclusion of the pact and which thereafter becomes an imperious obligation, one of the rigorous rules of the State. But Rousseau is a Genevan; he remembers that the city of Calvin is governed in large part by its pastors. The Encyclopedists substitute for this religion a State moral code. D'Holbach writes a *Natural Politics* but he also conceives an "Ethocracy," that is to say, the plan of a political system that is to be based upon the organization of a moral code, the teaching of the virtues necessary for the prosperity of the

State. In *Of the Mind* Helvétius demonstrates at length how an able government can model men's minds in accordance with the social moral code, how society may become whatever one wishes it to become: immoral and unhappy, moral and happy, the two terms in each case being practically synonymous. Mably is even more definite: "Is it not obvious that the reigning political code should make us love virtue, and that it is the only goal that should be aimed at by legislatures, laws, and magistrates? . . . The good legislator will be a moralist above all things." Diderot hardly constructed any definite political system; but he has spoken frequently of the moral code and always of a political moral code, a moral code that attempts to bring about the happiness of the greatest number.

The dominant principle of this social code is no longer: "Love your neighbor as yourself for the love of God" but "Love your neighbor as yourself for your own sake." Our egotism is directly interested in the happiness of others; every society is so constructed that the happiness of each one is intimately bound up with the greatest general happiness of society. If everybody thinks only of himself, this egotism inevitably brings about the ruin first of some,

then of more, then of all. So much has been
clearly pointed out on many occasions by
Diderot, d'Holbach, Mably, Turgot, Condorcet. But this concern for the welfare of one's
neighbor is by no means a mere interested
calculation or a mere logically constructed
argumentation. Moreover, its efficacy would
be quite uncertain and the social moral code
would crumble if it had only the demonstrations of wisdom to support it. Fortunately it
draws its force from a definite human instinct.
We suffer when we behold the misfortunes of
others; we are happy if they are happy, or at
least if they are no longer suffering. Rousseau insists upon this instinctive pity. Diderot
adopts the same viewpoint; he also believes,
more so perhaps than Rousseau, in the joy of
causing joy, in the happiness of gazing upon
happy faces. And all the rest of the philosophers believe in this concept or at least pre-
tend to do so: men like Mably, Condorcet,
L.-S. Mercier, Restif de la Bretonne, Delisle
de Sales, Raynal, and others.

We say of this type of morality that it is
altruistic. In the eighteenth century it is iden-
tified with *beneficence* and *humanity*. It is the
abbé de Saint-Pierre who creates the word
"beneficence." And there is general pride in his

having created the term (or rather having re-created it, for one finds it in Guez de Balzac). "A certain legislator," says Voltaire,

> Has created a word that is not in Vaugelas; [1]
> Beneficence, a gracious word. . . .

It is so pleasing a word indeed that it is frequently to be found in dissertations and treatises. "Everybody dabbled in economics," says Vaublanc; "one discussed nothing but philosophy, political economy, above all humanity and the means of bringing solace to good people." One comes upon works like the *Discourse on the Progress of Beneficence* or the *Complete Works of M. de Chamousset, Containing his Humanitarian, Beneficent, and Patriotic Projects*. Beneficence and humanity are to be found in tales, novels, and dramas. The description of the life of M. and Mme de Wolmar in the *Modern Héloïse* furnishes us with the model of an organization in which the squire and his lady assure the happiness of their servants and of the whole countryside and are rewarded with universal gratitude and love. Half the moral tales or dramas of Mar-

---

[1] [Author of *Remarks on the French Language* (1647), a treatise on usage in linguistic matters. Vaugelas restricted the vocabulary of "correct French" by condemning the use of vulgarisms, provincialisms, technical terms, and the like.]

montel, Baculard d'Arnaud, or Mercier—for example, the *Ordeals of Sentiment*, the *Recreations of the Sentimental*, the *Philosophical Dreams*—are "treatises on humanity" or on "beneficence." And the "touching" paintings of Greuze, the *Good Father*, the *Happy Family*, and the *Village Betrothal* are only commonplace illustrations of the sentiments that were dominating novels, poems, and dramas.

Moreover men did not content themselves with practising beneficence and humanity in imagination only. If there were happy families and contented mothers among people of slender means, there were also unhappy ones. There were famines in one province or another of France almost every year, and in certain cities or country districts a quarter of the inhabitants, or even more, were reduced to beggary. There is an effort, therefore, to find a remedy. There is an entire literature concerning the problem of mendicity: the problem is attacked in the writings of such men as Séguier de Saint-Brisson, who is a disciple of Rousseau, the abbé Baudeau, who is an economist, Moncrif, who is a poet, and many others. The Academy of Châlons offers a prize for the best monograph on the question; it is compelled to choose from a hundred competi-

tors. All this is still literature, but there is a
genuine attempt to introduce the doctrine in
real life. The beneficent squire, the village
bride and the village festival, the portrayal of
popular gratitude: these do not merely represent personages and scenes taken from the
comic opera or from the sentimental novel.
One comes upon them in real life; they constitute a fashion, a canon of taste. It is considered elegant to visit women in childbirth and
to succor the ill, just as it is to nurse one's in-
fant or to wear *poufs au sentiment*.[2] As in the
case of all fashions, this one is marred by de-
ceit and comedy: sincerity and hypocrisy seem
to exist side by side. For example, the *intendant* of Soissons, M. de Morfontaine, discovers
the ceremony of crowning a "rose-queen":
every year at Salency, in the Aisne district, a
chaste and industrious maiden of the people
is crowned the "rose-queen." There is general enthusiasm over this charming custom;
poets and romancers describe it in idyls and
tales. Soon, throughout all France, from Suresnes to Romainville or from Briquebec to
Monistrol, the crowning of "rose-queens" becomes a common occurrence, in fact some-

[2] [An elaborate feminine headdress of the eighteenth century.
It was designed in such a manner as to suggest one's leading
interest or hobby.]

what of an accessory of château life. At Canon
one finds the "festival of the good people." On
that occasion the squire of the district, amid
ceremonies of great pomp, suitably rewards
the "good father," the "good mother," the
"good son." People come thither even from
a distance and as if on a pilgrimage.

All this tearful and beribboned beneficence
of the eighteenth century has been rather discredited because of Greuze, the comic operas,
and the contrasting violence of the Revolution.
It was, however, often sincere and even profoundly so. Men really discovered, even if
they were pious, what one might call lay
charity, that which is not bestowed for the
sake of religion or duty or storing up merit,
but rather for the sheer joy of giving and of
sharing the happiness of others. And this
charity was very often effective. In the *Modern Héloïse* Rousseau had not concealed from
the Parisian ladies of the upper classes the
fact that he considered them immoral, not
overbeautiful, and mere slaves to ridiculous fashions. But he admitted that they did
possess at least one solid virtue: they left their
salons and their lovers not to read novels or
to write love letters, but to succor the needy,
to oblige people in want, to come to the aid of

the peasants of their estates. Almost all the gazettes, the *Mercury*, the *Literary Year*, the *Journal of Paris*, have a column in which they record "humane acts" either of heroism or of beneficence. Without doubt that means that these "acts" are being given due publicity; and it is not always certain that they are not entirely imaginary. But after all, one does not always offer a refuge to orphans or pay one's neighbor's taxes or share one's sheep with another merely in order to have oneself eulogized in the *Mercury*. A certain *Description of Humane and Beneficient Deeds or Historical Sketch of the Charities that are Carried on in Paris* (1769) is not only, as the provincial *Handbills* say, "interesting for the sentimentally inclined"; it is also interesting for historians, and it bears witness to an ingenuous and sincere desire to be helpful and kind. If we do not know much about the life of beneficent middle-class people who left no historians and of whom one catches a mere glimpse in the letters of Rousseau's correspondents, we do know a great deal of the life of certain great gentlemen like the duc de Ponthièvre or the duc de La Rochefoucald-Liancourt, whose mode of life was really shaped by their relations to their fellow men and not by the demands of social life. The sentimental moral code was no mere literary theme; it expressed itself in deeds and in progress.

The effect upon life.—Moreover, the significant trait of this sensibility was that it had a profound effect upon life and that it transformed practical habits quite as much as it did ideas. It is often quite difficult to follow the action and reaction of literature upon customs and *vice versa*; ideas are transformed into other ideas of which we find hardly any trace save among professional men of letters; we do not know how they were disseminated. But the sensibility of the eighteenth century fashioned realities of life that are direct proofs of the opinions that were held.

Thus it was that it transformed that longing for rest and leisure in which the profound needs of men are so clearly revealed. In the necessities of daily life it is life itself that dominates us; in repose we endeavor to mold it after our own heart's desire. Now, clearly, this desire in the eighteenth century ceased being merely rational and worldly.

First of all, there is a general affection—and a more sincere affection than of yore—for the country and for rustic life. It is true that

people sought repose in the country in the
seventeenth century; Boileau, for example,
had his little country house at Auteuil. But,
like all the rest, all that he sought therein was
tranquillity. When one had a château, one
might spend a few weeks or a few months
there every year. But rarely did one seek the
solitude of one's château, as did Mme de
Sévigné, to enjoy the silence of one's fine forest. It was merely considered the proper thing
to do; and one might even create a new species of mundane life in this retreat. On the
contrary, in the eighteenth century country
houses multiply, and not merely the sumptu-
ous dwellings of the financiers but "hermit-
ages," "lodges," "villas." They are constructed
not only on the hillocks that surround Paris
but throughout France, in the vicinity of all
the great cities, on the banks of all the rivers.
Everywhere memoirs, journals, itineraries, accounts of travelers express amazement at seeing ten of these country places where none
existed before. Without doubt not all who
have these country houses built are wont to
read the *Modern Héloïse* or Ossian; they go
to the country, perhaps, only to enjoy the fresh
air or the delights of fishing. But at times we
come to know exactly the type of pleasure that

these men seek; and even if they are more or less humble members of the middle class, they seek the typical pleasures of the sentimentally inclined. They go to the country to dream, to "let their hearts speak," to look at the moonlight, to enjoy the "melancholy of autumn." They are responsive to the poetry of far-off horizons and of solitary woods. They go on long walks, far beyond their country houses; and one may follow them as they depart, alone or in happy groups, for Suresnes, Meudon, Romainville, Montmorency. Or perhaps their pilgrimage takes them to the banks of the Loire, or the Marne, or the Rhone. Often enough, it is true, they seek only the open air, gay laughter, renewed appetite. But Manon Phlipon found something else; she found reverie, solitude, heartfelt emotions. And these humble, middle-class folk are representative of many others who, like Jean-Jacques, are "solitary pedestrians," who would lose themselves in "winding paths," in "somber woods," and "deserted valleys." Walking is no longer a corporeal joy and a delight in change of horizon; it becomes a humble and ecstatic sort of poetry.

This poetry finds expression in two fashions which of themselves would indicate that the atmosphere of life has been transformed: the newly acquired fondness for English gardens and for the mountains.

Of course gardens had always been as popular in France as elsewhere. But the gardens of the Renaissance are hardly more than tapestries of flowers upon which are arranged statues, vases, and carefully trimmed arbutus shrubs. The Nôtre and the gardens of Versailles enrich this tapestry with the amplitude and the majesty of great trees, large mirrors of water, vast lawns. But we still have here a rational and well-ordered nature. It is an architecture of verdure and of basins, that frames and prolongs that of a palace or a château. It is man who dominates nature and models it in accordance with his reflective art; its poetry is a well-regulated sort of poetry. In the second half of the eighteenth century, on the contrary, one is very often weary of order, and one distrusts reason. The order of the French garden seems to be a sort of treason against nature and a source of boredom. Then, toward 1750 one discovers the Chinese garden and the English garden. These gardens, which have been revealed by missionaries, by the translation of an English book by Chambers, then by travelers, architects, and French gardeners, no longer propose to improve upon nature; they are content to copy it. In nature everything is caprice, chance, fancy; there are no straight lines; there are no shears or rakes. And it is precisely for that reason that nature is fascinating and beautiful, because it delivers us from narrow restraints and narrow correctness. The "English" gardens, therefore, are to respect and to imitate the liberty of nature. The lanes will be laid out according to no fixed design; the trees will grow "as God wills"; the streams will be "capricious" and "torrential"; the declivities will be steep. If the brook lags, cascades will be dug for it; if the hill descends in a gentle slope, the slope will be made more precipitous; if the garden is on a plain, a mountain will be piled upon the plain, numberless carts being employed for the purpose. Instead of reducing nature to orderliness, art will force it to become disorderly and tumultuous.

Thus one will have a garden which is no longer merely English but "romantic" in the exact sense of the term. The word itself is English; and the English spelling is often utilized. At first the term is applied only to gardens. But it expresses very exactly what "sentimental souls" seek in nature; these gardens are to be the mirrors of their souls. The romantic garden of a marquis de Girardin is in reality a vast estate in which nature can abundantly incite "strong emotions," or "dreamy" and "tender emotions." The romantic garden is calculated to arouse enthusiasm, reverie, emotion. It has gorges, cascades, venerable forests, arid deserts; then hard by are cheerful valleys, peaceful streams, grazing herds. It is a veritable world of sensations rather than of thoughts. This romantic type of garden very soon becomes a fashion and an obsession. Rousseau has given a discreet example of it in the "Elysium" of his Julie de Wolmar; but there have been better visualizations and even realizations of the type before the *Modern Héloïse*.

There are illustrious romantic gardens: the one of the duc d'Orléans at Monceaux which has been sketched by Carmontelle and of which there still exist the artificial ruins of the naumachia; that of the comte d'Artois at Bagatelle where there is an artificial ruin, an artificial hill, and an artificial cascade; that of the painter, Watelet, at Moulin-Joli, where visitors may admire the willows bending over the stream and all the delicate refinements intended for the "feminine soul"; above all, that of Ermenonville, which will become the last refuge of Rousseau, where there is a "desert" which is *really* a desert, solitudes in a dark forest, an islet in a melancholy pond, and also an altar of reverie, a temple—unfinished—of philosophy, inscriptions upon the rocks, and, not long after Rousseau's arrival, the symbolical tomb of the great Jean-Jacques.

Rousseau had very little to do with the discovery and the progress of these gardens. But he did reveal one aspect of romantic nature: the mountain. Before 1750 hardly any one talks about the mountain, unless indeed it be to revile it. It is a region of were-wolves, and it spoils, so travelers say, the landscape and the charm of Lausanne or Neuchâtel. Not all the Swiss were of that opinion. Haller sang of the *Alps* and praised their landscapes as much as he did their inhabitants. His poem was translated in France (1750) and was widely read. But it was chiefly the *Modern Héloïse* that suddenly made Switzerland and the Swiss mountains fashionable. The scene of the novel is the shore of Lake Geneva at the very foot of the mountain peaks; the most pathetic episodes take place near the crags of Meillerie. Saint-Preux visits the lofty valleys of the Valais and the châlets that cling to the mountain sides. The celebrity won by the novel brings about the celebrity of the scenes that it describes. Travelers hasten to follow the footsteps of Julie, Saint-Preux, and Rousseau; they visit Geneva, Lausanne, Clarens, Vevey, Yverdon, Motiers-Travers, and the Valais. They eagerly question those who have known Jean-Jacques. They leave inscriptions everywhere. Later they come to Switzerland for its own sake, for the grace of its sloping fields, the mirror of its lakes, the charm of its châlets, for the "strong emotions" as well as the "tender emotions" that it can arouse, for the immensity of its horizons, the majesty of its summits, its vast silences, and the vertiginous depths of its abysses. One finds writers and society folk at Geneva, Neuchâtel, Lausanne. It is already considered fashionable to spend a few months in Vaud; the elegant ladies and the beaux have their amorous trysts there. Switzerland has become the country of lovers, of young married couples, of romantic souls, of "inconsolable souls."

Writers even improved upon Rousseau, who had not described the mountain of eternal snows and frozen solitudes; he had spoken only of the verdant mountain, of the Valais. People remembered what he had said of it in a delightful page of the *Modern Héloïse*, but they mounted much higher. There was tremendous interest in the works of the Swiss Alpine climbers, Bourrit and Saussure, who told of their attempts to scale the most formidable peaks and who vividly described the intoxication of the ascent. The notes that Ramond added to a translation of the account of a voyage by Coxe (1781) completed the conquest of the sentimentally inclined and of those who pretended to be so. The curious hastened to Saint-Gothard, to Grindelwald, to the glacier of the Rhone; they sought just that exalted meditation, those lofty flights of the soul that are to be the delight of the Romanticists. The mountain made a real poet of the mediocre Mercier, who had established himself at Neuchâtel. It gave the prose of Ramond the rhythm of poetry and something very closely akin to the inspiration of genius: "Profundity, majestic shades, I love to gaze upon you. Beside my abode on the slope of the Jura there is a torrent that leaps with frightful impetuosity; it flows into the dark shade of a forest of ancient fir trees . . . and my thoughts seem to lose themselves with the passing hours in the abyss of eternal things." "Everything tends to make one's meditations more profound, to give them the somber tinge and the sublime character that they acquire when the soul, taking the flight that makes it contemporary with all eras and all created beings, hovers over the abyss of time."

It is certain, then, that it was not unusual to live and even to die of sentiment before the Revolution; deliberately, complacently, and with a certain voluptuousness, even in suffering, even in self-destruction. Bernardin de Saint-Pierre, Benjamin Constant, Sénancour live or begin to live before the Revolution. They are professional men of letters, it is true, but men in whom the uneasy craving for adventure is no mere literary attitude. They search their innermost selves, they flee in search of new emotions from country to country, from horizon to horizon. The uneasiness that gnaws at their souls is a tormenting wound and not a mere pretext for declamation: "Sad plaything of the tempest that I am, I have been wafted from error to error . . . I have paid for days of happiness with months of misery . . . I suffered boredom in the midst of my pleasure and my sadness inevitably returned." It is Benjamin Constant who speaks thus and then it is Sénancour, but their accents are blended. They proved

moreover by the calamities of their own lives
that they believed in their literature. At times
men even died because of this excess of sentiment: "The unfortunate wretch," said Cam-
penon of his friend, Léonard, "had exhausted
the cup of sentiment. . . . His heart was already dead; and his vague uneasiness, increasing daily, became the all too certain foreboding of his impending death."

Nor were men of letters alone in making
sentiment the guide of their lives even if it
led them to suffering and despair. "Your
melancholy," said Ducis to Deleyre, "is past
all human remedy"; and he chose for him a
hermitage "near the woods, in the vicinity of
those broad pools in which the winds delight
is unloosing tempests . . . at the side of a
tortuous and most lugubrious valley." If
Deleyre is still somewhat of a man of
letters, we catch glimpses of others who are
hardly so. A certain comte de Montlosier
withdrew to his mountains of Auvergne to
experience the emotions described in *Isolation*
and the *Valley* long before Lamartine; to seat
himself in the twilight on the mountainside
and to contemplate in the distance the château
where his mistress had lived, the steeple that
overlooked her tomb. Fonvielle fled from col-

lege at an early age, adopted twenty different careers, was violently infatuated and as violently disillusioned, walked fifteen leagues at night to cast himself at the feet of a Platonic mistress whom he forgot a month later. Mme de Chastenay, as a young girl, lived more or less like the half-demented sister of Chateaubriand: "I was in a delirium . . . Everything was exalted within me. . . . Instead of sleeping I read incessantly." Mme de Cavaignac had a sister who wandered through the gardens "now reading aloud, now bursting into tears, or laughing wildly; her long, black hair flying in the wind, she recited the entire rôle of Armide." The future general, Thiébault, had never a thought of leading his regiments to the fray: "Sad and touching musical compositions, particularly those in the minor keys, made all my nerves vibrate by their analogy with a sort of melancholy that has formed the habitual state of my soul." On occasion this melancholy led to romantic despair. A young lady, a friend of Brissot, living in the humdrum peace of the city of Chartres, "weary of the world, of the baseness of others, of the despotism that was reigning everywhere . . . ended her own life at the age of seventeen." An unknown stranger blew out his brains at the tomb of Rousseau in Ermenonville, leaving certain adieux which constitute a sort of program of Romanticism: "I was of no country; all nations were indifferent to me. . . . Do not refuse a sepulcher to the wretched and melancholy dreamer in the place that he would choose. . . . Alas! How truly wretched are the sentimental! . . . It was unfortunate love, melancholy, delight in reverie, sensibility, that brought me to this sad state . . . for no man can long endure emotions such as these."

PART V

THE DIFFUSION OF THE NEW SPIRIT

CHAPTER I

THE RESISTANCE OF PUBLIC OPINION

In writing the history of the thought of a century it does not, or it should not, suffice to devote oneself exclusively to men of genius, or even to men of letters, or even to those who form the intellectual class. We are never sure of understanding men of genius as they would have us understand them, and we are sure not to understand them as their contemporaries did. Above all, as soon as we cease to shut ourselves up in pure art or in pure thought, as soon as we descend from æsthetic emotions or ideas to real life and to history, we must know precisely what passed from the speculation or from the emotion of the few into the life of the many: that is, we must consider the diffusion of new ideas. The history of this diffusion has not yet been written save in a few particulars. We propose to give an outline of it.[1]

[1] I intend to complete the history of this diffusion in a study of the *Intellectual Origins of the Revolution*.

There had been a tenacious resistance in many matters throughout the eighteenth century. Neither the philosophical spirit nor the sentimental spirit had conquered outright, or even profoundly stirred the nation. For society people, that is to say, for all those who are highborn or who are wealthy, philosophy and sentiment are two fashions among others; it is all a matter of amusing oneself and of thinking, or of seeming to think, like the others. And society folk are busied with many other amusements. The famous "joy in life" is not that of writing and thinking freely or of following the "impulses of one's heart." It consists of festivals of every description that *châtelains* strive to vary and that are organized by a species of professional entertainers, Moncrif, Collé, Carmontelle. There is the Ball of the Opera, which is illustrious, where even Louis XV or Marie-Antoinette ventures to appear; there are the *tenebræ* of the abbey of Longchamps; there are the promenades where great ladies and courtesans compare their carriages and their necklaces: the Queen's Drive, the Tuileries, the Boulevards; there are the places of gossip and pleasure: the Royal Palace, the Ranelagh, the Vauxhall, the fairs; there are the suppers where certain society folk practically keep open house and invite all those who can entertain.

Above all there are the fashions that succeed one another, that impose themselves and soon disappear in a sort of whirlwind: high heels and low heels, the monstrous perukes of the ladies, or their huge hoop-petticoats, the rhinoceros or the elephant. And then there are those extraordinary fads at the end of the century in which there is a survival and even an exaggeration of the most unreasonable and unphilosophical sort of spirit. In this "rational" century with its disdain for prejudices and superstition, superstition never ceased to flourish. Books on magic, sorcery and alchemy, secrets for conjuring up the devil and commanding nature are still numerous. There are many people who believe in watersprites and salamanders. The *Great Albert* and the *Little Albert* and many other cabalistic treatises are edited and reëdited, in fact until the very end of the century. And all this witchcraft, which after all had become rather unusual by now, suddenly became immensely popular together with the juggleries and the mysteries of the comte de Saint-Germain, Cagliostro, Saint-Martin and Mesmer. Mountebanks like Saint-Germain and Cagliostro often make the gravest of men believe that they command the powers of life and death and that they themselves are eternal. The tub of Mesmer has no fewer disciples than the philosophy of Voltaire and that of Jean-Jacques Rousseau. The end of the century witnesses a flowering of credulity as well as of the critical spirit and the religion of sentimentalism.

Upon leaving Paris and seeking information about the provincial nobility and the middle classes, one finds neither the *Great Albert* nor Cagliostro nor Mesmer. But in these classes are found firmly imbedded all the beliefs and the traditions of the past. At the château of the Talleyrands in Périgord, at that of the Montbareys in Auvergne, in the aristocratic *salons* of Poitiers there is as much delight in dancing, supping, and gambling as of yore; others live seriously and decorously and have no interest either in Voltaire or in Rousseau. There are hundreds of châteaux and *salons* in which one may find unquestioning obedience to King and Church. But this obedience is even more unconditioned among certain members of the middle classes. The great amusements, we might almost say the only amusements in certain cases,

are processions for which the entire city
gathers: the formal entry of a governor, a
prince, a bishop, or occasionally of the king
himself. We know this middle class well in its
higher and lower strata. Numberless lawyers,
merchants, notaries, and even farmers have
written notes on the events and at times on the
essential impressions of their lives in memoirs,
journals, and diaries. They never, or hardly
ever, dabble in politics. Almost the only exception is the occasion of Louis XV's dismissal of the parliaments; for that act concerned
local privileges and produced local disturb-
ances. Though these impromptu authors may
give numerous instances of want or of plenty,
they hardly ever mention "abuses," "privileges," "necessary liberties." A Malebaysse
notes that in order to see the elephant one must
pay twenty-four *sous* for the first row and
twelve for the second; and one third of the
space that he devotes to the elephants amply
suffices for the mention, without comment of
any sort, of the death of Louis XV. A Le-
prince d'Ardenay in Mans, a Cavillier in
Boulogne, a professor of the University of
Dijon are educated and even intellectually
curious people. They read, they meet, they
discuss. But they do not say a word about Vol-

taire, Diderot, Rousseau, the *Encyclopedia*, political and religious disputes. Seguin, advocate in the Parliament of Lyons, gravely relates that the cardinal de Tencin has had incestuous intercourse with his sister and that she has borne him a son called "the sieur d'Ardinberg." That is all that he knows of d'Alembert, the director of the *Encyclopedia*. And most people know still less.

In all these simple souls, so faithfully devoted to the past, religion—and a very strict and unquestioning sort of religion—evidently has an important rôle. It is true that incredulity makes some progress even among such as these. But for a long time it is a menace, no more. Even among the more exalted of the nobility there are certain devout and even mystic souls: the marquis de Castellane, the princesse de Montbarey, the duc de Croy, the duc de Penthièvre, and many others. In the provinces religion often maintains its profound influence. Montgaillard complains that he found only catechisms in the châteaux of the Lauraguais. The comte d'Allonville is persuaded that Voltaire saw the demons of hell before his death. The middle classes make no effort to think more philosophically than their masters. A great number of families practise

their religion with scrupulous piety, that of
Mme Vigée-Lebrun, that of Frenilly, that
of Carnot, that of Joubert. François
Gilbert regularly makes an examination of
his conscience. Gauthier de Brécy detests the
"impious philosophers." Temisier, a former
ironmonger, is no ignoramus; he buys books,
but they are books directed against the phi-
losphers; he belongs to six pious lay orders.
Duminy spends his leisure time transcribing
thirty-three Christmas carols, the life of Saint
Mary of Egypt, and that of the beatified
Father Dom Robert Mauvielle. Contemporary travelers who have visited these provincial places generally affirm that the new spirit
is more or less unknown. At Autun the inhabitants regularly attend mass and vespers. The
same is true in Doué, Valence, and in all
Provence. On the very eve of the Revolution,
one still reckons the inhabitants of a parish
by the number of communicants.

Life itself often follows the traditional
routine. Until the very end of the eighteenth
century men often live as their ancestors lived
before them; theirs is a humble life, well-regulated, without ambition, without curiosity.
Even well-to-do families have their meals in
the kitchen; bridal dresses and costumes are

transmitted from generation to generation; custom forbids the wives of notaries, surgeons, and merchants to wear topknots or furbelows of vivid colors. Their pleasures consist of luncheons in their gardens, or in the village inn in the winter. They do their household work in the kitchen. "Two fires in a middle-class house," says Grosley of Troyes, "were then an unknown luxury." At Autun the women spin wool; and this wool suffices to clothe the father, the mother, and even the children of the family—that is, when the children do not wear the cast-off clothes of their elders. Everywhere one finds the mode of life of "the good old times."

Among most of the members of the middle class therefore traditions maintain their strength until the Revolution. And yet they do not entirely maintain their strength. Even in the provinces, even among more or less humble folk one feels that little by little the good old customs of the past are being supplanted by more modern customs. The taste for luxury, for diversion, for gambling, for comedy, spreads from the wealthy *salons* to the homes of the middle-class burghers, from Paris to the most remote of the provinces. At Troyes there is a "revolution" in public morals. At

Autun, after the meeting of the States General of Burgundy in 1763, "luxury is all the rage." At Saint-Antonin and at Grasse the inhabitants continue their "vigils," in which the husks of grapes are discarded after the last pressing; but now to these "vigils" are added dancing and gambling for high stakes. Everywhere an attempt is made to organize balls, concerts, society theaters. At Thouars there is "perfect ignorance of history and literature." But there is no ignorance of the dictates of fashion, for one finds concerts, *soirées dansantes*, and even "witty converse." The burghers are beginning to think that they may possess as abundant wit as their betters. And that road leads to "philosophy."

CHAPTER II

THE STRUGGLE AGAINST AUTHORITY

Historical note.—Beaumarchais was born in Paris in 1732. The son of a watchmaker, he soon abandoned his father's calling in search of adventure. He gave lessons on the harp to the daughters of Louis XV, busied himself in the financial affairs of Pâris-Duverney, disentangled or possibly entangled, diplomatic, commercial, and family affairs in Spain. He was involved in certain serious lawsuits, in which he had the knack of interesting public opinion (notably the suit of the comte de La Blache, heir of Pâris-Duverney, and that of one of the judges who condemned him in the La Blache affair). His infinitely witty *Memoirs,* directed against Goëzman, amused all Paris. He was later commissioned by the court to follow up and, if possible, to silence certain authors who, taking advantage of foreign residence, were writing libels against the royal family. He also organized a company to furnish arms to the American revolutionists. He produced the *Barber of Seville* in 1775 and the *Marriage of Figaro* in 1784. Suspected and exiled during the Revolution, he returned to France in 1796 and died in 1799.

The road to philosophy was beset with obstacles. The philosophers might think like skeptics and infidels; but it was very difficult for them to communicate their skepticism and their infidelity. The political authorities and the Church were in alliance and they had formidable weapons at their disposal. No book, no journal, no printed matter whatsoever could appear without an "authorization," without the permission of the censors. Terrible penalties were provided for authors, printers, and hawkers of books that might be not even prohibited but merely not authorized. An edict of the king dating from April, 1757, expressly renews the old penalty, which was death for authors or printers. Edicts of 1764, 1767, and 1785 prohibit the publication of anything concerning finances, religious questions, legislation, jurisprudence. The penalties against blasphemy and impious speech, penalties entailing even mutilation and death, supplement the laws on bookselling. Of course all these edicts were never strictly applied. But nevertheless during almost the entire century blasphemers were being sent to the galleys for life, sacrilegious persons were being deprived of their hands or even being burned alive; the chevalier de la Barre had his hand and his head cut off. In 1768 a hawker was condemned to five years in the galleys and his wife was sentenced to life imprisonment for having sold *Christianity Exposed* and the *Man with Forty Sous*. Neither d'Holbach, who wrote the first of these works, nor Voltaire, who wrote the second, was in any danger of the galleys or of life imprisonment; but they ran the risk of the Bastille or Vincennes and if one did not exactly "rot" in these dungeons, a stay in either of them was not really pleasant. Diderot, Voltaire, d'Alembert, and Helvétius held them in great awe. In fact Voltaire, Diderot, Morellet, and Marmontel unwillingly visited these places and had no desire to return. There was genuine danger in being too boldly philosophical.

Moreover, the authorities acted effectually against the philosophers, or at least they attempted to do so. Until the year 1748 the recognized "wits" of the time were not particularly molested. A few books, including the *Philosophical Letters* of Voltaire, were condemned; there were a few raids of the police against printers, a few confiscations, a few imprisonments. But on the whole these pamphleteers were held in but slight esteem; and the police were particularly occupied in ferreting out the printing establishments, the books, the pamphlets, and the journals of the Jansenists. It was not until about 1750 that the

Government and the Church began to observe that the philosophers constituted a "sect" and a "party," and that their designs were to be feared. The *Philosophical Thought*s of Diderot were condemned (1746) by the Parliament. Yet the philosophy contained therein was timorous and availed itself of subterfuge; and Diderot was as yet an inconsequential sort of person, who was closely watched by his curate and by the police commissioner of his district. The *Morals* of Toussaint caused a graver scandal, for Toussaint was a well-known lawyer and a man occupying a prominent position. Moreover the doctrine expressed in the *Morals* is openly worldly and impious. Toussaint demonstrates that religion is without doubt quite respectable, but that neither morality nor society has need of religion. One may be a very respectable person and one may govern very well without concerning oneself about revelation and the catechism. The book was condemned and Toussaint was forced into exile (1748). But then scandals of the same sort multiplied. The *Spirit of the Laws* of Montesquieu studied the various forms of government without assigning any place whatsoever to revealed religion and without paying due respect to the monarchy by divine right. A certain Méhégan published a history of *Zoroaster* (1751) which was merely an insolent mockery of Christianity and a defense of natural religion. Under the pretext of studying the blind, in his *Letters on the Blind*, Diderot professed the keenest sympathy for the atheism of the blind Saunderson. Buffon published the first three volumes of his *Natural History*, which acquired great popularity. This book contained a history of the earth that, according to Buffon's contemporaries, "contradicted Genesis in every particular." It was not easy to publicly censure Montesquieu, president of the Parliament of Guyenne; after all, his only crime had been to ignore religion. It was not altogether easy to condemn M. de Buffon, a man of standing in his province; but at least he was censured and he was obliged to publish a very humble declaration, in which he submitted to the wisdom of the Sorbonne and accepted the history of the world according to Genesis. Méhégan and Diderot, petty writers, were imprisoned in the Bastille and in Vincennes, respectively, as an example to their fellows. And every one appeared to be satisfied.

Yet the philosophers confessed themselves

neither convinced nor vanquished. And they began to set up against authority and tradition an implement of warfare the peaceful appearance of which had at first aroused no suspicion. In 1751 there appeared the first volume of the *Encyclopedia*. It was nothing more than a dictionary of the sciences, and a dozen of these dictionaries, though less ambitious, of course, had already appeared: that is to say, the *Encyclopedia* merely represented a fashionable sort of enterprise. Without doubt it was a rationalized dictionary, but it was firmly believed that faith and reason could be reconciled. Without doubt the leaders of the enterprise were two philosophers, Diderot and d'Alembert. However, they would be watched; they would be compelled to conduct themselves properly. The publishers therefore obtained the authorization and privilege. Yet following the appearance of the very first volumes it was evident that these philosophers were not to be trusted. In spite of the theologians who were supposed to have an eye upon the enterprise, in spite of the pious orthodoxy of certain leading articles, all sorts of adroit insinuations led the reader toward doubt and impious negation. Immediately after some inoffensive article on an obscure topic of mythology or of natural history there would be another article, mocking credulity, condemning fanaticism, and clearly suggesting that Christianity, like any other religion, lived on credulity and reigned by fanaticism. Protests arose. Finally the hesitation of the authorities was overcome because of one incident. In 1751 the abbé de Prades, a friend of Diderot and a collaborator in the *Encyclopedia*, maintained in the Sorbonne a theological thesis in which nobody at first saw anything except legitimate theology. It was authorized and then accepted. Then it was perceived that this thesis was advancing manifestly heretical propositions; it became known, or it was believed, at any rate, that Diderot had something to do with the matter. The *Encyclopedia* paid for the audacity of the abbé de Prades; it was suppressed in 1752.

But the collaborators on the *Encyclopedia* had defenders, among them Mme de Pompadour; besides, great material interests were at stake. Mme de Pompadour, the Sorbonne, and the subscribers came to an agreement; the authorities deliberately overlooked a great deal. The *Encyclopedia* was no longer put on sale publicly but it was still being printed. Moreover, it persisted in adroitly serving the ideas of the philosophers and not those of tradition. Three theologians officially superintended the enterprise; but they were lacking in patience and perspicacity. By skillful cross-references, by allusions, by articles which outwardly were eminently respectable but in which embarrassing problems were attacked with the utmost frankness, Diderot, Morellet, and others taught men to doubt and to deny. The adversaries of the philosophers sought another pretext to condemn the *Encyclopedia*; they found it in the publication of Helvétius' *Of the Mind*.

Of the Mind apparently did not concern itself with religion. It contented itself with studying the fashion in which our ideas, habits, and customs can come into being. Yet it was clear that for Helvétius all our ideas come from our sensations and that in our sensations there are merely the actions and the reactions of matter, that all our habits are derived from our experiences and that religions are habits, just as much so as anything else. Now this materialistic book appeared with the name of its author, with an authorization that the censor had given inadvertently. There was a tremendous scandal. The censor was dismissed; Helvétius, in order to avoid persecution, was forced to sign and to publish three very humble retractions. *Of the Mind* was solemnly censured and condemned. Furthermore, this condemnation was put to account. Helvétius was an Encyclopedist; it was affirmed that the *Encyclopedia* in its entirety led to the same impious conclusions as Helvétius' work. The enemies of the philosophers insisted and threatened. In short, the Council of State revoked the authorization in 1759; the printing of the work was henceforth prohibited; philosophy was "annihilated."

Still the philosophers and, more generally speaking, all those who professed to say exactly what they thought did not confess defeat. They had been accustomed for a long time to the ruses of warfare and to that peculiar form of warfare by ambuscade in which the authorities were easily outwitted. The printing establishments were restricted in number and were closely watched. But now clandestine printing establishments multiply. The enterprise has its risks and the penalties are cruel; as late as 1757 a certain abbé de Capmartin is condemned to nine years in the galleys. On the other hand the profits are great; and for every printing plant that is confiscated, two spring up. Besides, even if

audacious printers are lacking, there are innumerable manuscript copies. The impious
books that were to be printed in the second
half of the century circulated in manuscript
in the first half: *Heaven Open to All Men* by
Father Cuppée, the *Testament of the Curate
Meslier*, the *Treatise of the Three Impostors*,
and so forth. Copies are numerous—even to-
day there exist a goodly number of them—
and Voltaire observes that in his time there
are more than a hundred copies of the *Curate
Meslier* in Paris. And then foreign printers
are perfectly free to print in French certain
works which the French government does not
fancy. Thus the most audaciously philosophical works are published in London, Amster-
dam, Leyden, Geneva. All that remains to be
done is to bring these works secretly into
France and Paris. Of course the customs officials are on their guard. There are police
raids. The government has its spies, and occasionally the entire cargo of a ship is examined.
But there are a hundred ways of outwitting
the authorities. Clerks and customs officials
are bribed. Besides, all those who have some
state rank have the right to pass the custom-
house or the tollgate without being obliged to
have their baggage or their carriages ex-

amined; and the carriage of the *intendant* or of the prince must not be searched even if its owner is not inside. Thus Rousseau receives the proofs of the *Modern Héloïse* and of *Émile* without any disturbing incident and without his even having to pay the cost of carriage; it is thus, through the good offices of Catherine II of Russia, that Falconet receives the *Testament of the Curate Meslier*. Of course, favors of this sort are generally well paid for. Prohibited books and manuscripts are very expensive in the first half of the century. A *Memorial for Abraham Chaumeix* sells for as much as six louis, *Émile* for two. However, the prices are ultimately reduced. Hawkers offer the *Sacerdotal Imposture* for two crowns, and *Superstition Unmasked* for twenty francs. After 1770 the price is generally no longer reckoned in louis or crowns but in francs; censorship becomes so nonchalant that the prohibited books are sold almost publicly. The Swiss, Fauche-Borel, while in Paris in 1780 easily disposes of the works printed by his father, works like the *History of the Two Indies* by Raynal. Even in Versailles and the very streets through which the monarch passes, bookshops keep on their rear shelves the *Morals* of Toussaint, the *Virgin Maid* or the *Philosophical Dictionary* of Voltaire, the *Christianity Exposed* of d'Holbach.

Against the Sorbonne, the Parliament, the threat of the galleys, and even that of death the philosophers have as an ally that most powerful of all forces, public opinion. This includes the "opinion" of the *salons*—and one is not considered to be a fashionable gentleman unless one frequents them. Soon the philosophers have the support of the Academy itself. These allies intrigue with patient skill, and before long the party of the philosophers is triumphant over that of the defenders of tradition. Soon it becomes elegant to scorn "prejudice," "superstition," and "fanaticism." Soon the conviction becomes general that there can be no human dignity without liberty of thought, and no social order without tolerance. Thus it is that magistrates themselves become the accomplices of the philosophers against the interest of the authorities whom they are supposed to represent. It is thanks to Malesherbes, the director of the book trade, that Rousseau can have the *Modern Héloïse* and *Émile* printed. The manuscripts and the folios of the *Encyclopedia* are hidden in Malesherbes' house while the printers' premises are being searched. Brissot has given us a

picturesque account of the mere pretense of
prosecution in the case of authors. The inspector of the book trade who had been
charged with Brissot's arrest came to warn
him politely to depart, for on the morrow he
would come to arrest him. The inspector sold
through his wife the books that he had come
to confiscate. Moreover, it is not entirely certain that Malesherbes and the others were de-
linquent in their duties or were betraying the
interests of the authorities. Prosecution no
longer frightened anybody; it merely made
the government ridiculous and assured its victims of a reputation. The lawyer, Barbier,
who was not very fond of the philosophers,
was convinced that it was quite wrong to make
so much of the thesis of the abbé de Prades:
"the affair should have been hushed up" and
"the faithful should not have been allowed to
become curious." When the abbé Morellet
was sentenced to the Bastille for six months,
his friends urged him to seek consolation in
the fact that "those six months in the Bastille
would be an excellent recommendation and
would inevitably assure him success." Morellet was ultimately convinced that his friends
were right; he became successful and so did
several others who shared his fate.

Thus at the very moment when the authorities seem to triumph and the *Encyclopedia* seems to be definitely suppressed, the battle is decided in favor of the philosophers and its episodes henceforth become a series of reverses for the Sorbonne and the Parliament. The adversaries of the philosophers redouble their attacks. The lawyer, Moreau, publishes his *Outline of the History of the Cacouacs*; Palissot produces the *Philosophers*; the *Literary Year* of Fréron teems with adroit polemics. But Moreau and Palissot are mediocre literary figures. Fréron, who is intelligent and more to be feared, is not supported; he is even prosecuted on occasion. Consequently all the attacks directed by the Parliament, by the Sorbonne, and by the bishops and archbishops come to naught. The *Encyclopedia* is still being printed by tacit permission. When it is completed, the only favor that the authorities ask of the "condemned" printers is that Geneva be indicated as the place of publication instead of Paris; and the Parisian subscribers are to obtain their copies of the work in the suburbs of the city and not in the city itself. The other philosophical works have much the same history. Those which are openly impious and which are printed or composed by d'Holbach or Naigeon, works like the *Philosoph-ical Soldiers*, the *Sacerdotal Imposture*, *Christianity Exposed*, and so forth, are sold rather easily in surreptitious fashion. D'Hol-bach and Naigeon, who keep their secret rather skillfully, live at Paris without being molested. The same comedy takes place in the case of the other works. First there is a scan-dal. The Sorbonne or the Parliament or per-haps both carefully deliberate about the mat-ter: a list of passages to be censured is drawn up. The author is exiled for a few months or perhaps spends a few days in prison. He be-comes famous and his book is eagerly sought. So it is in the case of Marmontel's *Belisarius*, which defends tolerance. Thirty-seven propo-sitions are condemned; the Faculty of Theol-ogy censures the book (1767). The censure is greeted with bursts of laughter and the Sor-bonne receives the order to refrain from fur-ther discussion of the matter. The *Philosophy of Nature* of Delisle de Sales is condemned in 1777 after a notorious law suit and the author is imprisoned. But the Parliament reverses the verdict and Delisle de Sales leaves his prison in triumph. For his part, Buffon detests "the-ological wrangling." In publishing his *Stud-ies of Nature* he takes precautions and is ex-

ceedingly polite to the theologians. Yet the
latter realize that their theology is hardly consistent with the doctrines of Buffon. They
meet; but they are given to understand that
they are to be good enough to hold their
peace; and they are silent. In 1781 Raynal
publishes a new edition of the *Philosophical
History of the Two Indies*. It is enriched with
violent diatribes against the religion that has
bathed the two Indies in blood. The book is
condemned and Raynal is forced into exile.
But the work is immensely popular; and soon
Raynal returns triumphantly to France. The
Marriage of Figaro by Beaumarchais is a very
impertinent play, particularly in its attitude
toward the nobility and its privileges. Its production is prohibited. Yet Beaumarchais is
not prevented from giving private readings
from the play and from thus conquering public opinion. Public opinion demands that the
play be produced: the authorities yield. At
the last moment Louis XVI opposes his veto;
he likewise yields. The production is a triumph. Beaumarchais takes advantage of it and
writes a rather insolent letter to the *Journal
of Paris*. He is arrested and imprisoned; but
at the end of a few days he is freed amid a
perfect storm of applause.

Thus from 1760, more decidedly from 1770, and above all toward 1780, practically no obstacle is presented to the dissemination of the new spirit. There is no longer any real struggle between the brute force of authority and the world of ideas. The battle is between varying opinions: traditions on the one hand, skepticism, negation, and revolt on the other. We must now follow the history of this battle of ideas.

CHAPTER III

THE DISSEMINATION OF
HIGHER EDUCATION

"In Spain," says the marquis d'Argenson in
1752, "ignorance still fetters men and pre-
vents them from reasoning. The same situation existed in France for a long time." But
times have changed in the eighteenth century
in France. Even if one does not always know
what men are reasoning about, it is quite certain nevertheless that they have acquired a
taste for reasoning and that learning has
spread with astonishing rapidity.

Primary education is widely discussed in
the eighteenth century, as is attested by numerous and precise documents. As a result, if
there are still certain strata of the populace
that are ignorant, schools are multiplying almost everywhere. Often as many as seventy
per cent, sometimes more, of the male population can sign their names. But with some
exceptions neither the political authorities

nor the philosophers endeavor to disseminate this instruction. Almost all the philosophers distrust the "populace" and prefer that it occupy its arms rather than its wit. Consequently the primary schools are in the hands of the clergy. The subjects taught are reading, writing, arithmetic, the catechism, sacred history: this instruction has only practical or pious aims. It is evident therefore that primary education cannot serve as a means of culture nor does it inculcate even the beginnings of intellectual curiosity.

But the same cannot be said for the higher education which is given in the colleges and which is prolonged or renewed by reading and discussion. Voltaire, d'Argenson, and some others, to be sure, affirm that men do not read in the provinces, and that the matters they discuss are such things as the composition of a sermon or the recipe for a tart. But we have abundant evidence to the opposite effect. In fact d'Argenson contradicts himself: "Today every one reads his *Gazette of Paris*, even in the provinces. Men are continually arguing about politics, rightly or wrongly, but at any rate it occupies men's minds." If d'Argenson speaks only of that particular province that he happens to know, others confirm his judgment. La Beaumelle is quite astonished to find among the twelve or fifteen hundred inhabitants of Vigan "men of letters who are endowed with abundant wit." At Nérac, at Saint-Antonin in the Rouergue, at Agen, at Valenciennes, even in the farms and among petty village burghers there are "highly educated people" who buy many books, subscribe to two or three gazettes, read the *Natural History* of Buffon, the *Encyclopedia,* the *Dialogues on Wheat* of Galiani. This evidence is quite scattered of course, as is inevitable, since modest folk do not generally transmit their history to posterity. But it is supported by testimony of a more general character.

Books, journals, and gazettes cost a great deal; consequently, reading groups are formed in order to buy them. Almost everywhere there are societies where people meet in order to seek "respectable diversion": to talk about the affairs of the city or about their own affairs, to play backgammon or chess. But toward 1770 or 1780 "respectable diversion" includes readings; and readings necessarily and almost inevitably bring about discussion. "Entertainment groups" thus become literary societies. In Paris itself there are hardly any of these groups outside the Masonic lodges. But there

are founded courses of higher education that
have a striking vogue: the *Museum* of Court
de Gébelin, the scientific *Museum* of Pilâtre de
Rosier, the *Lyceum*, where the lecturers are
Garat, La Harpe, Parcieux, Fourcroy. In
1777 Junker, a royal censor, gives a public
course in political science two or three times
a week. In the provinces there are reading
societies at Caen, Laval, Saint-Antonin,
Castres, Mans, and so on, where one reads
"novels and public documents"; at Agen,
where the society is called *Politics*, "its only
defect is that it has become rather tumultuous;
besides, one must put up with the most ridiculous political reasoning and conjecture." The
casino of Nice, where newspapers are provided for the members, is founded in 1786. At
Bordeaux a *Museum* is founded in 1783. Its
motto is "liberty, equality"; it is rapidly taking the place intellectually of the University,
which has been rapidly degenerating. Other
cities establish or attempt to establish similar
societies. At times, as at Mans, they gather together men of different stations in life. Elsewhere membership is restricted; the societies
cater to the aristocratic or the wealthy. But
other societies are being founded. At Agen,
besides the "association of all the most distin-

guished inhabitants," there is one for "procurators and middle-class folk," and another for the "ambitious members of the lower classes." At Saint-Brieuc one "literary chamber" gathers together the nobility, the canons, and the wealthy merchants; another, the middle-class folk; they discuss "politics, the reform of existing abuses, equality of taxation." Public libraries are opened or founded. At Verdun there is the library of the *Premonstrants*, where one may find "almost all the works prohibited by monarchic despotism or by the Court of Rome," Locke, Voltaire, Rousseau, Boulanger, Helvétius, Mably; at Boulogne-sur-Mer there is a reading room where one may read the "French, English, and Dutch gazettes and newspapers" and where one may borrow three books a month; at Bordeaux there is the library of the Academy, and so on. In almost all the provinces there now appear *Gazettes* or *Handbills*: at La Rochelle, Poitiers, Caen, Rheims, Toulouse, Troyes, Nancy, Bourgues. Very anodyne journals they are indeed; they merely copy the *Handbill of Paris*, give some local news, indicate real estate values, and so forth. Still they do carry announcements of books; and these books are analyzed. And they are

often supplemented by journals in manuscript
form which conceal nothing and are very impertinent. The correspondence of Grimm, of
Métra, of La Harpe, of Bachaumont is intended exclusively or chiefly for foreign con-
sumption. But the correspondence of others is
received by curious people of Caen, of Bordeaux, and elsewhere. Finally there are the
Academies. Not every one could belong to
the French Academy; consequently the idea
was conceived toward the beginning of the
eighteenth century of founding provincial
academies in order to reflect a little glory upon the scholars of Dijon, Lyons, Bordeaux,
and other places. Throughout the eighteenth
century these academies are being founded
almost everywhere; there are at least forty of
them, and not only in the large cities but at
Bayeux, Villefranche, Cherbourg, Soissons,
La Rochelle. Very often they are not merely
obscure coteries of old gentlemen. They are of
wide reputation in the provinces and sometimes they acquire national renown. The
Mercury gives an account of their meetings;
the provincial *Handbills* announce their
prizes. Rousseau and later Buffon cause the
Academy of Dijon to become famous. When
Raynal pays a visit to that of Lyons, the audi-

ence is so great that it is found necessary to hold the meeting in a larger hall.

Moreover, the activity of these academies is great. Dozens of monographs are read every year; almost two thousand are prepared for the Academy of Rouen in less than fifty years. There are numerous competitors for every prize that is offered. Of course, there is a great deal of rhetoric in all these readings and scientific papers; and academic discourses, odes, and elegies are as popular as ever. Such ideas as are expressed are as yet very mild and very respectful; for an academy is created by letters patent, and imprudence may prove fatal to it. At Montauban and at Béziers the members attend mass before the public meeting. The discourses submitted to the Academy at Montauban must end with a "short prayer in honor of Jesus Christ" and must be signed by two doctors of theology. The motto of the Academic Society of Cherbourg is "religion and honor." Discourses and monographs are often bitterly hostile to the "false philosophy" of the Encyclopedists; they vehemently condemn the spirit of revolt and impiety.

And yet, as has been said in the case of the Academy of Agen, "these activities betoken an accretion of knowledge, and that is a great deal for a city that hardly knew how to read forty years before." This knowledge is experimental and realistic and it replaces rhetoric and mere wit. At least half the subjects of academic prizes are concerned with agricultural, commercial, and industrial problems bearing on wines, wheat, oil, mineral water, mills, epidemics, and the like. The research is local in nature and is intended for the agriculture, the commerce, and the industry of the provinces. Often the very philosophy of the Encyclopedists is involved, the spirit of critical inquiry. At Metz one discusses *Of the Mind* by Helvétius, *Of Nature* by Robinet, the *Social Contract* by Rousseau. One does not approve of these works; yet one reads them and causes others to read them. At Lyons the abbé Millot praises English philosophy; it has "dissipated the obscurity and the extravagances of peripateticism . . . and established experimental physics." At the Academy of Amiens, Rousseau is eulogized; at the Floral Games of Toulouse, a eulogy of Bayle is proposed, later one of Rousseau. At Caen the abbé Le Moigne denounces the "excesses of fanaticism" that caused the murder of Ramus and the imprisonment of Bacon and

Galileo. And the Academy of Nancy excludes the abbé Ferlet from its competition, "alleging," writes Ferlet, "that he was attacking certain Encyclopedists too vehemently."

There is general interest in social problems and abuses, occasionally even in such abuses as seem to reflect upon the existing social order; there is great interest in depopulation, the ravages of luxury, the theories of Montesquieu, the sumptuary laws, the penalty of death (discussed by three Academies), the education of the people. Rouen discusses the nature of penalties, criminal procedure, the trading nobility, the unification of customs, public education. Dijon awards a prize to Brissot, who protests against the tragic disproportion between crimes and penalties. The Floral Games vaunt "the greatness and importance" of the American Revolution; and the Academy of Amiens seeks the means of suppressing the various guilds.

In short, there is everywhere a "veritable thirst for knowledge." It is evident that persons like Geneviève de Malboissière, Mme Roland, and Brissot are not altogether exceptional. Geneviève de Malboissière is rich, well-born, beautiful, popular. But she spends her days in study. She knows English and

Italian. At the age of fifteen and a half she rereads all of Vergil, Tasso, Ariosto; she has sundry discussions with Hume; she takes lessons in natural history and in physics; she begins the study of German and Spanish; she can translate Greek fluently. At the age of seventeen, in a single day she completes a German theme, composes an Italian theme and a Spanish theme, rereads the first volume of the *Roman Revolutions* of Vertot, finishes the first volume of Robertson, and reads twenty-two pages of Buffon. Manon Phlipon, the future Mme Roland, who is the daughter of an engraver, studies physics and mathematics, reads the abbé Nollet, Réaumur, Bonnet, Clairault, ransacks the library of the abbé Le Jay, devours Pluche, Rollin, Crevier, Father d'Orléans, Saint-Réal, Vertot, Mézeray, then Montesquieu, Locke, Burlamaquai, Nicole, Pope, all of Voltaire, Boulanger, the marquis d'Argens, Helvétius, Malebranche, Leibnitz, Raynal, Bayle, Morelly, Rousseau. This reading program is overambitious, perhaps, and decidedly desultory, but it proves that the daughter of a humble engraver had access to all these books. Indeed it is rather easy for the sons of modest folk to pursue studies that will enable them to "take the decisive step":

to abandon their engraving, their pastry shops, or even their farms in order to become lawyers, procurators, or priests. That of course is not peculiarly characteristic of the eighteenth century. For a long time there had been scholarships in all the colleges; in the seventeenth century the holders of these scholarships generally became priests, as the founders of these scholarships had desired. Fewer of them become priests in the eighteenth century; but they finish their studies and they are generally successful. When they return to Agen or elsewhere after successfully presenting their theses, the village notables await their entry into the village; they are seated at a solemn banquet with aldermen and magistrates. Mahérault, the son of a baker of Le Mans, wins an honorable mention in the general competition at the college of Louis-le-Grand. Brissot is the son of an innkeeper who has seventeen children; yet young Brissot studies with the master of a boarding school, then at college; and he completes his studies brilliantly. The father of Marmontel is a humble tailor of the little city of Bord in Limousin; yet Marmontel finds the means to continue his studies at Mauriac, then at Toulouse; finally he becomes a member of the French Academy. It may be said indeed that, toward the close of the eighteenth century, education is available for almost all, and for every purpose.

CHAPTER IV

THE GENERAL INFLUENCE
OF PHILOSOPHY

Education might have been one of the
weapons of tradition; it might have persisted
in the ideas of the past and it might have in-
culcated these ideas in the students who were
under its sway. But education too becomes
susceptible to new ideas. We have seen that
Latin had been compelled to renounce its
privileges, that a more modern and a more
realistic education had been demanded and
even introduced timidly. But now it is philosophy itself, it is the "School" that is being
transformed. The old scholastic philosophy,
glorying in its seven or eight centuries of disputes and renown, begins to retreat before the
violent attacks of its adversaries. Diderot and
the *Encyclopedia* overwhelm it with mockery. It appears to them the height of nonsense
to inquire "whether being be univocal with
respect to substance and accident" or whether

it lie in the power of God to become an onion or a pumpkin. D'Argens, Savérien, d'Alembert, Helvétius, Voltaire, and others laugh heartily at problems such as these. Descartes, who was under the ban at the beginning of the eighteenth century, is soon tolerated; Cartesian evidence and reasoning take the place of scholastic logic. Then comes Newton, and with him the experimental spirit gains ground, even imposes itself. Later even Locke and Condillac find a place in the curriculum of the schools. In 1751 Loménie de Brienne maintains in the Sorbonne a thesis in which he refutes the innate ideas of Descartes and defends the sensism of Locke. The Oratorians, particularly at Troyes and Le Mans, are unfaithful to scholasticism and follow Locke and Condillac; it becomes necessary for bishops to censure, and to impose orthodox academic manuals.

When one studies these manuals one evidently finds nothing that suggests the *Philosophical Thoughts* or the *Treatise on Sensations*. The form of these manuals is almost always scholastic and the conclusions never range beyond a vague Cartesianism. The manual of Dagoumer is used until the end of the

century, and as the provincial *Handbills* affirm—and they are decidedly not philosophical—it represents the work of "an old ath-
lete of the School"; that is, of the scholastic
school. Other manuals published in the second half of the century (those of Mazéas,
Hauchecorne, Le Ridant, Vallat, Caron, and
others) are friendly to Descartes or even entirely Cartesian: "*Methodus cartesiana op-
tima est, et ad recte philosophandum neces-
saria*," [1] says Le Ridant. But they do not go
beyond Descartes; they even refute Newton on
occasion; they are composed in Latin and are
arranged after the scholastic fashion. Others,
however, are more audacious. Martinet publishes his *Logic* and Migeot his *Philosophiæ
Elementa*[2]; and these works repudiate the
"needlessly difficult, obscure, useless, and dis-
couraging elements of the ancient philosophies." In 1771 Seguy publishes a *Philoso-
phia ad usum scholarum accomodata.*[3] The
Mercury considers it a classic and congratu-
lates the author on having spoken amiably of
Leibnitz, Locke, and the authors of the *Ency-*

---

[1] ["The Cartesian method is the best, and essential to valid
philosophical speculation."]
[2] ["Elements of Philosophy."]
[3] ["Philosophy adapted for school use."]

clopedia, and on having "profited" by their discoveries. And indeed Seguy often cites— and sometimes with approval—Montesquieu, Rousseau, and the *opus famosum*[4] of Locke. Finally Beguin and the abbé Jurain are even bolder. Beguin, teaching at the college of Louis-le-Grand, observes the form of scholastic exposition but protests against the scholastic spirit. He teaches experimental physics, chemistry, natural history, after the fashion of Nollet, Romé de Lisle, Macquer, Rouelle. He ardently eulogizes Newton, Bacon, and Locke. In the town hall of Rheims the abbé Jurat gives lessons in mathematics, "French philosophy," and "experimental physics"; he "does not waste much time with metaphysics"; he repudiates the "barbarous methods of the Scholastics" and he adopts the methods of Malebranche, Newton, and Locke.

If the spirit of Bacon, Locke, and Condillac penetrates the very fortresses of scholasticism, the colleges and seminaries, it is not astonishing that it so often wins the allegiance of those who are not composing metaphysical manuals. Among the nobility as well as among the middle classes the philosophers, of course, have determined adversaries or hesitant

---

[4] ["Famous work": i. e., the *Essay on Human Understanding*.]

readers who often do not know whether to applaud or to become indignant. Men like Aguesseau, Montbarey, and the duc de Ponthièvre are not particularly fond of the "philosophical sect." Hardy, who is a respectable citizen, Narbonne, who is a police commissioner, Piron and Collé, who are fashionable wits, have no marked sympathy for Voltaire, Diderot, and d'Alembert; Narbonne would like to imprison Voltaire in the Bastille for the rest of his life. Others are converted and then repent; they yield to secret curiosity and sympathy, and then become uneasy and reproach themselves. Marais is very pious; he is fond neither of Voltaire, who is a "rascally Zoïlus and a serpent," nor of his philosophy, which is "frightful and worthy of being consigned to the flames." The lawyer, Barbier, is constantly fearing for the security of his money and his income; he is "obliged to believe" in a miracle when a procession passes. For the marquis d'Argenson, Voltaire, Diderot, Rousseau, and the rest are only riffraff; he detests the spirit of revolt and irreligion and the audacity of petty folk who meddle with ideas. And yet Marais is the enthusiastic and almost devout friend of Bayle; he "builds a temple to him"; he ridi-

cules the miracles of Marie Alacoque[5]; he
admires the *Henriade*. Barbier considers that
the works of Montesquieu are masterpieces
and thinks that the abbé de Prades is a youth
of "great merit and superior education" and
that Morellet is "a superior man." He is constantly seeking all the works that are suspected
or that are under the ban: the *Morals*, the
Sermon of the Fifty, the *Encyclopedia*. D'Argenson shows the utmost scorn for bigotry,
hypocrisy, the stupidity and the gossiping of
theologians, the disputes between the Jansenists and the Jesuits. And it is he who gives
shelter to the abbé de Prades and enables him
to leave France after the scandal of his thesis.

Marais, Barbier, and d'Argenson write before 1760. At that time, and particularly after
that time, the philosophers have admirers who
give themselves whole-heartedly to their
cause. Mme de Frénilly, who is pious, is
"fascinated" and wants her son to be able to
say to the sons of his sons: "I have seen Voltaire." The mother of Chancellor Pasquier is
so devout that she does not want to have her
daughter vaccinated for fear of appearing to

[5] [Marguerite (later called Marie) Alacoque (1647-1690), who
made a vow of perpetual chastity at the age of four, became a
nun in 1762. She subjected herself to severe mortification of the
flesh; and Christ is said to have appeared to her frequently.
She was beatified in 1864 by a decree of Pope Pius IX.]

mistrust Providence; yet she is on friendly terms with J.-J. Rousseau, who has been condemned by the Sorbonne and the archbishop of Paris. It is well known that the return of Voltaire to Paris was the occasion of a mighty apotheosis. Even the grandfather of Mme de Villeneuve-Arifat, "who was not a man to follow the general current of the times," goes with his wife to see the great man. Mme du Hausset remarks that "after reaching a certain age" women no longer become devout but philosophical.

For the philosophers have the *salons* in their favor. In the first half of the century the *salons* are, above all, "clearing houses of wit"; they are frequented by the philosophers, Voltaire, Fontenelle, Montesquieu, Rousseau. But Mme de Lambert, Mme de Tencin, Mme Geoffrin, and even Mme du Deffand are not fond of discussing the powers that be. One may talk at their *salons* of gallantry, of literature, of the fine arts, or of the sciences; one must not discuss religion or politics. Conditions change in the second half of the century. At the *salons* of Mlle de Lespinasse, Mme Helvétius, and the baron d'Holbach, every one says what he pleases and in the manner that appears best to him. *Salons* multiply

and almost all boast of being "philosophical."
Even at those of the marquise de Castellane,
who is devout, and Mme Necker, who is
quite pious, one may meet d'Alembert, Condorcet, Raynal, Diderot, Mably. Other *salons*
yield completely to the prevalent trend of the
times. There are the *salons* of Mme de la
Briche, where one meets Saint-Lambert and
Morellet, of the duchesse de Choiseul, of the
maréchale de Luxembourg, of the comtesse de
Ségur, of the duchesse de Grammont, where
one may see Raynal, Mably, and Marmontel,
where one reads Helvétius, Rousseau, Voltaire, Diderot; there are the *hôtels* of the
duchesse d'Enville and the duc de la Rochefoucauld, where one may find men like
d'Alembert, Condorcet, Raynal, Turgot, Gui-
bert, and such liberals as Choiseul, Rohan,
Maurepas, Beauvau, Castries, Chauvelin.
There are more modest *salons*: at that of the
father of Dufort de Cheverny one sees Voltaire, Fontenelle, and Turgot. Maury, Lemierre, and Rulhière frequent the *salon* of M.
de Nicolaï. Mably is the "hierophant" of the
salon of the grandmother of Mme de Chastenay; her mother receives d'Alembert, Marmontel, and Condorcet.

Those who have no *salons* in which to receive the philosophers read their books. English travelers, Talleyrand, Montbarey, the duc de Croÿ, and others recognize that the new ideas have won over members of the bar and public officials. Dutens says that it is all "a fashionable mania," and he knows a rich shoemaker who has become a philosopher. P. Lamare, the secretary of the Benedictine monk, Dom Goujet, reads the *Encyclopedia*. N. Bergasse, pious, cautious, and respectful, admires Voltaire and visits Rousseau. Sicaire Rousseau, squire of le Jarthe in Périgord, is a gentleman who believes in his religion; and yet, with the lawyer, Coeuilhe, he subscribes to the *Encyclopedic Journal*. Laurent de Franquières of Grenoble goes to visit Voltaire at Ferney. In his youth the poet, Chabanon, has mystical crises; he thinks, as his curate does, that it is a crime to go to the theater. And yet he visits Ferney several times and on one occasion remains there for six months.

Philosophy also exercised a notable influence upon Freemasonry. The rôle of Freemasonry was a very important one in the eighteenth century, especially after 1775; on the eve of the Revolution it had organized nearly seven hundred lodges in France. Indeed an attempt has been made to demonstrate that the Revolution was its work and that its chieftains had connived at a vast "philosophical" and atheistic plot to overthrow monarchies and churches throughout Europe in the name of "free thought." But there exists no serious proof of this plot; no doubt it was conjured up by a few German mystics. It found no echo in France. On the contrary the archives of the various lodges prove that they were inspired by a very respectful and prudent spirit. They got along very well with the ecclesiastical authorities and with all authorities. Many respected priests and large numbers of the nobility belonged to these lodges. Moreover their principles were mystic rather than rational and philosophical. The unifying impulse that bound their members together was the faith in the Masonic tenets rather than inclination toward the critical spirit. The Masons believed in "the great architect of the universe," in humanity, in beneficence. But they also believed in certain doctrines that were equally dear to the philosophers and to "sentimental souls"; that is, in tolerance and equality. This equality was even put into practice to a certain extent. The lodges were very rarely entirely democratic; people of the humblest classes were not admitted. But the nobility and the middle classes really met on an equal footing.

Thus the Masonic spirit and the philosophical spirit, derived from different sources, found a common meeting ground; many lodges, especially in Paris, were the allies of the philosophers. In the provinces the penetration of philosophy was slower. A great number of the archives seem to indicate that the Masons sought in their lodges only the naïve pleasures of strange ceremonies, banquets, vanity, or the joys of "sensibility" or "humanity." But without suspecting it they were in a philosophical frame of mind; they were taught and they firmly believed that all men are brothers. If they had no desire to obtain liberty by violent means, they aspired to equality and fraternity. Thereby in 1788 and 1789 the lodges became an admirable means of propaganda for the ideas of the Third Estate as against those of the privileged orders. They were not at all revolutionary before 1788; but they constituted the fissures through which the revolutionary spirit was rapidly to infiltrate throughout all France.

Toward 1780 the philosophers might be feared and detested; but they could not be ignored. On their side they had the prestige

of fashion and of popularity. We have now
only to follow the consequences of their triumph.

CHAPTER V

THE PROGRESS OF THE CRITICAL
SPIRIT AND OF INCREDULITY

The first consequence of the triumph of the philosophers was very often the crumbling of that foundation of religious faith and monarchical faith that for so many centuries had made the French faithful subjects of their kings and their curates. There is much evidence, either approving or condemnatory in nature, to indicate clearly the rapid progress of incredulity. As early as 1722 the Princess Palatine indicates this progress, and later Denesle, Diderot, and many others add their testimony to the same effect. There are not a hundred persons in Paris "who believe in the Lord." Pyrrhonism is an imperious fashion; "one launches unconditionally into materialism." "Everywhere," says an obscure novelist in 1779, "one hears only invectives and cries of fury against the ministers of the Church; they are summoned before the tribunal of

reason and are required to prove religion as
one would demonstrate a mathematical truth.
. . . The entire kingdom wishes to read and
to seek wisdom in the schools of the new
sages; with three hundred pages of lies, sarcasm, and gross violence these neophytes of
learning would silence the most learned defenders of revelation, and give the lie to a
religion that is six thousand years old." The
evidence in the provinces is as conclusive as
the general evidence. At Langres the bishops
inveigh against the progress of philosophy.
At Lyons the lawyer, Seguin, affirms that
"Catholicism has degenerated into an almost
universal deism; faith is quite extinct and I
verily believe that the end of the world is
approaching." At Châlons "religion has almost disappeared." At Rouen it is true that
"religion has suffered incomparably less than
it has elsewhere"; but that is due perhaps to
"conservatism."

These are opinions and impressions in
which there may be a certain amount of ill
humor and exaggeration. But numerous facts
confirm these impressions. In a single year,
from 1752 to 1753, the number of communicants at Saint-Sulpice decreases from 4,200 to
3,000. At the Sunday mass at Ainay-le-Châ-

teau, at Nantes, and elsewhere there are constant scandals and irreverent acts which arouse bitter complaints. At the hour of mass at Saint-André de Fontenay certain reprobates play nine-pins and amuse themselves with "scandalous dances." The edicts prohibiting work and commercial transactions on the Sabbath are increasingly ignored. There are numberless condemnations, sentences, and edicts of the police and the Parliaments at Rambervilliers, Caen, Rouen, Moulins. Even the processions, which were the glory, entertainment, and spiritual communion of the towns, are neglected little by little. The village societies no longer turn out in a body for these processions. Complaints to that effect are made at Gray, at Buglose, in the Landes, at Caen, at Châlons. Even in the colleges, where religious instruction is considered paramount, faith, or at least the external practice of religion, is disappearing. At the college of Plessis, Duveyrier does not once confess or take communion in a period of twenty-two months. At Felletin the practice of the duties of religion is very imperfect and not a few pupils are absent from mass. At Juilly confession "is a sort of recreation" and it is "an occasion for playing pranks." The transition from indifference or irony to hatred is an easy one. As early as 1734 Father Castet asserted that "a number of would-be wits and society people would be quite content to see what they call the monastic riffraff treated with contempt; and they would even like to censure the ecclesiastical hierarchy, pope and bishops included." Twenty years later, if one is to believe d'Argenson, this rebellion has become a violent and general revolt; the hatred against the priests "reaches its highest pitch." Barbier confirms the statement of d'Argenson. In the provinces an anonymous writer hails the coming of a time "when the world will be rid of all soldiers, minions of the law, priests, and courtiers." And at Toulouse in 1781 it is decided that the four scholarships of the college of Foix which had been reserved for priests are henceforth to be awarded only to laymen.

It is probable that philosophers are not always responsible for this indifference and this impiety, either directly or indirectly. Men had not required the stimulus afforded by the *Encyclopedia*, or Fontenelle, or Bayle in giving up their religion or in denying its veracity. When the duc du Maine, J.-B. Rousseau, Piron, and certain others eat meat on a

Friday, it is not because of their "philosophy," for Piron detests the philosophers. The marquise de Prie dies without the sacraments and "very insolently"; she "wants to throw the curate out of the window." The duchesse de Mazarin at the moment of death "rejects the sacraments." These two ladies had not busied themselves overmuch with reasoning. In the provinces many of those who do not practice their religion are without doubt, like the parents of Henriette de Montbielle, not philosophical and impious but "non-believers and indifferent."

On the whole, however, the progress of incredulity keeps pace with that of philosophy. And there is precise evidence to the effect that indifference and hostility are often rational, as much so as in the case of Voltaire, d'Holbach, and Raynal. Even Barbier and the marquis d'Argenson, who do not respect the insolence of the philosophers, are at heart in sympathy with their ideas. D'Argenson considers that their books are "indecent libels," but in his *Memoirs* he adopts the very tone of these "libels." For him the Sorbonne is nothing but a rotting carcass. The *Encyclopedia* is a "great and useful book"; and d'Argenson dreams of a time when the people shall "banish all priests, all revelation, all mysteries" and when they shall "worship a God who is self-evident because of His great and good works." In the case of others the influence of philosophical reading is still more evident. When the comte Beugnot follows the courses of the *Lyceum* he is not opposed to the philosophy of the eighteenth century, "far from it." Yet with certain companions he has a rather lively altercation with La Harpe: "we asked him to suppress certain harsh allusions to religion which he introduced with no discernible motive or excuse in certain excellent literary discussions." Joubert is on terms of friendship with Diderot, Guillart de Beaurieu, and L.-S. Mercier. Carnot becomes a deist after having studied both theology and the writings of the philosophers; Rousseau is his master; he pays him a visit. Others, more violent, are among those who, to quote Beugnot, "make the war upon the *Infamous Thing*[1] the general program of the day." "I dined to-day," says Wal-

---

[1] [An epithet directed by the Encyclopedists against the Church. Voltaire in particular used the phrase "Écrasez l'Infâme!" ("Crush the Infamous Thing!") in his letters in much the same spirit in which Cato the Censor was wont to proffer the vindictive "Ceterum censeo Carthago esse delendam" ("For the rest I think that Carthage must be destroyed").

pole, "with five or six savants; and although all the domestics were present to serve us, the conversation was far less reserved, even in the discussion of the Old Testament, than I would have suffered at my own table in England, even if but one lackey were present." One of the friends of the comte de Tressan defends La Mettrie's *Man-Machine*. M. de Fréville is "a sort of public professor of atheism"; in 1782 he boasts of his beliefs publicly, in a café of the rue de Richelieu. It is possible that this atheism penetrated even to the lower classes. In 1782 there were at the Salpêtrière two women who were living "with men and who were bound by no other tie than love." They are the proselytes of "an atheistic system that is quite widespread, so it is claimed. . . . These women say that there is no God; that the love of virtue is of itself sufficient to make good citizens; that man should have no other aim in life than this same love of virtue; and that if they are to be persecuted for following this manner of thinking, it will redound to their glory; it is most pleasing to suffer for virtue."

We know in its precise details the case of Mme Roland's philosophical conversion; her letters enable us to follow it month by month and sometimes day by day. At seventeen she is still pious and almost mystical; at great length and very methodically she demonstrates her belief for her own benefit, borrowing her arguments from her readings, from Bossuet, Fénelon, and Pascal. Then she has a crisis of doubt; her reason is attacked first of all: "I admire the manner in which God holds me to religion through pure sentiment, while my mind alone would cause me to reject it; I reason and I doubt, but I feel and I submit." Then while she is still reasoning, and in order to reason more effectively, she reads "all of Voltaire," Boulanger, the marquis d'Argens, Helvétius, Raynal, even Morelly's *Code of Nature* and d'Holbach's *System of Nature*. She does not approve of the atheism of Morelly and d'Holbach; she adopts the philosophical system of the man whom she reads after the rest but who is her real master, J.-J. Rousseau. The crisis is precipitated. "I do not desire to break off, although I hardly believe any more"; and then she finds that she no longer believes at all. And for her own benefit she demonstrates her incredulity by employing the arguments of Voltaire, d'Holbach, or Rousseau, just as she had proved her faith to herself with the aid of Bossuet, Fénelon, and Pascal.

It is probable that philosophical incredulity is particularly prevalent at Paris. Yet the evidence attests that it wins over the provinces quite rapidly and thoroughly. Everywhere one reads the books of the philosophers, even if one is pious. The *Encyclopedia* is bought by middle-class families of Angers, Laval, Agen. They know a great deal about the disputes involving the philosophers. "The thesis of the abbé de Prades," writes a correspondent of Grosley, "causes as much of a hubbub here as at Troyes." At Saint-Germain Duveyrier scornfully remembers the theological zeal of boarding school masters and mistresses. They make mere children of ten or twelve argue "as though they were embryonic doctors raised to the dignity of sophists." One may well imagine these controversies between boy and girl "doctors" of the same age. The boys win the debates because they shout louder; and to celebrate their triumph they play hide-and-seek, puss-in-the-corner, and saddle-my-nag in the chapel. Rejecting this theology, Duveyrier is drawn to philosophy: "It appeared to me impossible to believe what I did not understand; it seemed to me to be a shameful and ridiculous lie to affirm that I believed without understanding; the fact that I was required to do so was a mystery even more impenetrable than the others." Everywhere one begins to reason as did the youthful Duveyrier. M. de Conzié, the friend of Rousseau, has in his library fifty-seven volumes of "Voltaire, Diderot, and their disciples." At Langres Diderot met "certain men who had very decided and clear opinions concerning the notable prejudices of the time; and—a fact that caused me genuine pleasure—they are considered to be perfectly respectable people." In Lorraine "pernicious books are widely disseminated"; the *châtelaine* of Sommerville is "a philosophical prude." "Every little city has its party of young philosophers, who are aggressively impious. At Vézelise they oblige the priests of the deanship to transfer their synod to Sion in order not to be molested." Sermons now consist only of "philosophical maxims. . . . There is no *Ave Maria*; there is no reading of Holy Scripture, there is nothing about the Fathers of the Church."

For philosophy has won over even the

clergy, and not only the superior hierarchy of the clergy and the secular abbés but also not a few serious and moderate priests and seminary students. At Saint-Sulpice, it is true, they refute the vicar of Savoy, Buffon, the "false philosophical concepts of Diderot," and many other productions of the same type. But the refutations are not always entirely satisfactory, and the abbé Baston claims that even Saint-Sulpice is infected with the philosophical spirit. The abbé Legrand makes a profession of faith to Mme Roland that "is quite like that of the vicar of Savoy"; it is he who brings her the *Modern Héloïse*. The abbé de Bonnaire, an Oratorian of Troyes, reveals himself at his death as "an avowed and notorious deist." The abbé Bouisset of Bayeux, the tutor of the children of the baron de Fontette, is on friendly terms with d'Alembert, d'Holbach, and Diderot. Dom Mulot, the prior of a Benedictine monastery at Chartres, pronounces a sermon "in which the name of Christ is not mentioned" and he is proud of having made "an audience of bigots swallow it all down." At Saint-Dié a deacon reads *Of the Mind* during a procession and even in church. The seminarists are almost all "deists and Epicureans." A seminarist of Toul has "all the works of J.-J. Rousseau in his trunk."

These documents are not unique. They confirm what d'Argenson felt impelled to observe as early as 1751. Revealed religion is not definitely in ruins; but "everywhere its foundations are crumbling."

Chapter VI

POLITICAL UNREST

The deliberate shaking of religious foundations was evidently dangerous to the State. The critical spirit shown in destroying the respect for religion was lessening the respect for every other type of institution, and particularly the respect for the monarchy. The French monarchy was really definitely doomed only when an important part of the population no longer thought it beneficent or inevitable. A revolution took place in men's minds, or at least in the minds of many, before the Revolution of 1789 actually broke out. And it is possible to follow very clearly the progress of this revolution in public opinion.

It was not general by any means. In 1789 a great number of Frenchmen who were neither dunces nor simpletons believed in the King and awaited the remedy for their misfortunes only from his kindness and wisdom. Until about 1750 this attachment of the nation to its King was general and profound. The illness which in 1744 imperiled the life of Louis XV while he was at Metz caused universal sorrow, and his recovery caused as much rejoicing as a veritable resurrection. This love was already far less deep at the time of the criminal attempt of Damiens. Then quite rapidly it became indifference and even disdain. But until the very end there were still some who were obstinately faithful to the monarchical idea. Hardy detests Maupeou and all those who dismissed the Parliaments, but he attests his love "for the sacred person of the King," and he would not abandon it "for an income of a hundred thousand crowns." Barbier, who has no sense of respect, has a genuine hatred and horror for anything resembling "a detestable scheme of revolt." More generally speaking, when one reads the hundreds of memoirs, journals, and diaries of the eighteenth century one observes how little concern there is about problems of general politics, except in the case of a few great names. People live as their fathers lived before them and they do not appear to believe that they could live otherwise. The disputes that interest them are local affairs and concern aldermen: for example, the construction of a fountain, the question of precedence in a procession.

Yet even those who do not reason are suffering. Even if one does not discuss the prevalent abuses and the necessity for reform in the State, one must needs feel the weight of these abuses and one must see that the State is not perfect. "There is here," writes Barbier in 1760, "a great agitation in men's minds with respect to the Government. One must admit in very truth that famine and the scarcity of money, the misery in the country districts, and the multiplicity of taxes make one suspect that depredation is going on in the administration of the finances and that apparently nothing can be done about the matter." Let us add to that statement another that Barbier makes about "the pilfering of the court people" and the pilfering and the insolence of practically all those belonging to the privileged classes. Inevitably there will be a feeling of anger and a desire for vengeance. Even respectful and timid men like Hardy are impelled to avow that "one groans at seeing unpunished" crimes like that of the duc de Fronsac, who is guilty of kidnaping and rape, or the first public crime of the marquis de Sade, and that "one is indignant when a young servant girl of twenty-two is hanged for a trivial domestic theft." The consequence of all this is that even if one may continue to respect and venerate the King himself when he has virtues like those of Louis XVI, nobody now respects the nobility. The nobility of the higher rank makes a public display of its vices, its adulteries, its mistresses, its insolent luxury, its booty in the form of pensions and benefices, whereas the nobility of the provinces very often is ruined, degenerates, is a prey to utter misery, and is compelled to perform the most menial tasks. One may indeed resign oneself to the existence of privileges; but there is no one, if one excepts those who enjoy these privileges, who believes that they constitute a recompense and a right.

Above all, one cannot resign oneself to famine and to revolt. There had always been famines and revolts in France, even in the most flourishing period of monarchical unity and order. There were riots in the streets of Paris in the reign of Louis XIV because of the kidnaping of children by the police or because of the high cost of bread. But toward 1750 famines and the revolts caused by famine multiply. Perhaps the people were no more wretched than before. The really careful in-

vestigations of the subject that have been carried on hitherto have all been local and at
times mutually contradictory. But certainly
people were less resigned, more inclined to
snatch up axes and scythes, and to pillage.
From one year to another, from one month to
another, the price of bread was subject to the
most violent fluctuations, ranging in price
from a *sou* and a half a pound to five *sous*. At
times a half or even two thirds of the population were reduced to beggary. The sufferers
ate grass; then they gathered in bands and violently attacked flour mills, bakeries, shops in
the town or city. Everywhere, at Paris, Versailles, Caen, Valenciennes, Strasbourg, Toulouse, Clermont, Dijon, Nancy, Arles, Agen,
Tours, Cherbourg, Rouen, Grenoble, Cette,
and so on, diaries are full of frightened accounts of these popular uprisings. And these
are not transitory outbursts of wrath, caused
by empty stomachs and quite forgotten as soon
as the insurgents are no longer hungry. The
diarists are particularly frightened at the
placards that the rebels post and at the principles that these placards proclaim. There is
no mere repetition of those innumerable coup-
lets, ballads, and ironical and insolent epigrams which multiply in the eighteenth

century and which have caused it to be said
that in France every tumult ends peaceably
with song or verse. These placards, on the contrary, are really challenges and the announce-
ment of a deliberate and concerted revolt. The
authorities have to tear them down everywhere, in Paris, even in the Louvre itself,
from the doors of churches, in the Luxembourg, at Versailles, "in the very chamber of
the king," at Caen, at Grenoble, at Troyes. At
Grenoble the following truculent appeal is
posted: "O, enslaved and servile people of
France! Scorning the laws, one deprives you
of your property in order to forge chains for
you. Will you endure it all?" And at Troyes
one may read: "We demand our daily bread.
. . . It is better to live without law than without bread. No one can deny that!"

The dismissal of the Parliaments clearly
manifested the prevalent state of unrest. The
Parliaments were neither revolutionary nor
republican nor even in favor of reform. At
bottom they were merely defending their own
privileges and their prestige. But they were
menaced by the ministers of the king; they resisted; they suffered. The meetings of the
Parliament of Paris were suspended in 1753,
and the members of the Parliament were ex-

iled or imprisoned. Then, after alternate triumph and defeat for the royal will, Maupeou suppressed all the Parliaments in 1771 and replaced them by superior councils. Throughout all France, or very nearly so, the old Parliaments are regretted; the councilors of Maupeou are scoffed at; there is determined resistance against their authority. When the old Parliaments return, at the death of Louis XV, there is universal rejoicing; there are solemn celebrations, parades, fireworks.

In all this unrest, turmoil, and revolt there is really nothing that is directly philosophical. Neither the discontented, nor the seditious, nor their placards invoke the authority of Montesquieu, Voltaire, the *Encyclopedia*, or J.-J. Rousseau. As we have shown, not one of the philosophers could be considered a revolutionist, and they all profoundly distrusted popular government and even liberty. It seems quite certain that the Revolution was in one respect the unreasoning protest against misery and the spontaneous revolt against suffering. Yet philosophy did play a very definite rôle. It taught neither revolution nor democracy. But it transformed men's minds; it made them lose the habit of respect for tradition; it made them apt to reflect upon revolution and democracy. It cleared the soil in which the seeds of new harvests could germinate.

A characteristic example is furnished by the violent uprising of the Norman nobility in 1771. The nobles were certainly not revolutionists nor were they reformers; they merely refused to pay a certain tax (the Third Estate had nothing to do with the movement). Nor was the uprising very audacious. As soon as the authorities became stern and imprisoned the leaders, the rank and file vied in proffering the most humble supplications. Yet these nobles claimed that they were supported by the people, whose misery at that time was very great. They printed pamphlets that a Morelly or a Sylvain Maréchal might well have signed: "Let us now hear the monarch, that is, the agent of the nation, say to those men from whom he holds his authority: 'I want no resistance; that is to say, I do not want you to think. . . . I do not want you to be men; far less, citizens, but I do want you to be perfectly servile.'"

The reception accorded the American Revolution also curiously reflects the half-conscious evolution of men's minds and the penetration of philosophical ideas into poli-

tics. At the outset, French public opinion is by
no means won over to the cause of the American Revolution; moreover, it is powerfully
influenced by English propaganda. It is men
of influence (and particularly Vergennes)
who shape public opinion and partly at least
orient it, while calculating the political benefits accruing in the event of an American victory. But the moment that public opinion has
definitely come to a decision, it sympathizes
not merely with one people in its struggle with
another but with ideas, with a political philosophy. The philosopher, Morellet, did not
understand this enthusiasm; but he noted that
everybody "wishes to drink a toast to the liberty of the Americans, to liberty of conscience,
to freedom of commerce." The success of
Franklin, who is the hero of the *salons*, is due
to the fact that he appears to be a "philosopher" who unites the wit of Voltaire with
the simplicity of Rousseau. The "sentimental
souls," the disciples of Rousseau, find themselves for once in perfect agreement with the
"dialecticians of liberty." One is touched by
the evangelical life of the Quakers and by the
happiness and the industry of the clearers of
virgin forests. And this enthusiasm, in which
are blended the love for ideas and the unrea-

soning impulses of the heart, soon wins the entire nation. All the younger nobility wish to depart with La Fayette to fight for a people that knows nothing of nobility and that proclaims equality. The students of the colleges take a passionate interest in the American cause. At the college of Plessis, La Fayette is the hero of the hour. At the college of Juilly, Father Petit deals as much with "the American war and the exploits of Washington and La Fayette as he does with the odes of Horace and the orations of Cicero." "At the convent," says Mme de Fars-Fausselandry," "the cause of the Americans seemed ours; we were proud of their victories." Neither the middle classes nor the lower classes are in ignorance of these victories. At Clermont-Ferrand the Declaration of Independence is celebrated by public rejoicings. A peasant of Provence, Gargaz by name, comes to Paris on foot, to cast himself at the feet of Franklin. And one of the first societies in which revolutionary ideas are adopted is the Society of the Friends of the Negroes, an organization obviously inspired by the doctrines of the Quakers.

Other evidence shows that little by little people are acquiring the habit of associating reforms, liberty, and philosophy. That is evident in the case of the "philosophical" *salons* in which one listens to Franklin, Raynal, Turgot, Necker, Mably, and Condorcet. It is certain, even in the case of those nobles who hasten to be present at the private readings of the *Marriage of Figaro*, at M. de Vaudreuil's, at M. de Liancourt's, at Mme de Vaines', at M. d'Anzely's, and so on. It is certain in the case of the provinces, where people seem to know all about what the philosophers do and publish. Very daring pamphlets in manuscript circulate at Bordeaux, Lectoure, and elsewhere. Those which the governor of Normandy receives and which he does not keep for his own use indicate the success of the *Observations on the History of France* by Mably, the *Ingenuous Man* by Voltaire, *Belisarius*, the *Philosophical History* by Raynal, the *Friend of the Laws*, the *Catechism of the Citizen*, the *Disadvantages of Feudal Rights*, in short, all those works which in demanding reforms develop ideas and speak in the name of principles.

"I will confess to you," writes Mably in June, 1789, "that I find the Third Estate, whose defender I have been and still am, a trifle radical in its views and its principles."

Even before 1789 the Third Estate and the nobility itself certainly had very definite views
in politics. And if these views were not revolutionary, they were in part at least philosophical.

CONCLUSION

If one may believe that there is a definite
break in the evolution of the eighteenth century and that the upheaval of the Revolution
represents something really new, there is on
the other hand no definite beginning. The
philosophical spirit appears as early as the
seventeenth century; and there are unmistakable resemblances between a Saint-Evremond or a Fontenelle and a Duclos or a
Chamfort. Yet a profound transformation in
French thought certainly does take place between 1670 and 1770. Taken all in all the
contemporaries of Boileau, Racine, and Bossuet would have seemed quite alien to those of
Bernardin de Saint-Pierre, Raynal, and Marmontel. Even those who apparently are defending the same cause, who resist the philosophy and detest the heresies of Rousseau,
often adopt the viewpoint of a Rousseau or
even a Voltaire rather than that of a Pascal
or a Bossuet. We have observed that an abbé
Pluche, an abbé Nollet, or an abbé Fromageot

often discourses about reason, observation, and experience like a Buffon or a Diderot. One of the most celebrated works of Catholic apologetics toward the end of the eighteenth century is a work by the abbé Gérard, the *Count of Valmont, or the Errors of Reason,* a book that runs through ten editions. Certain illustrations of his, and the explanatory legends: "The natural law or the rule of reason—The love of order and of the common weal—The contemplation of nature," might well be inserted without changing a single detail in a book by Delisle de Sales, J.-J. Rousseau, Voltaire, or Diderot.

At all events, these men of the end of the eighteenth century are infinitely closer to those of the end of the nineteenth than to those of the corresponding period of the seventeenth. One may say that they knew all the forms of our contemporary thought and that they even measured their consequences and understood their contradictions. They carried the spirit of inquiry to its most audacious limits; they exercised without restraint the rights of rational criticism. If they had not as clear and methodical an idea of historical criticism and of the reconstruction of the past as the historians and the exegetical scholars

of the nineteenth century, at least they understood the essential requirements of these
studies and sketched their methodology. They
saw with the greatest clarity that logical and
abstract truth, geometrical and mathematical
reason, are human creations and that they do
not necessarily constitute all of reality or even,
perhaps, any considerable portion of it. They
understood as clearly as our modern scholars
the value of experimental truth, the laws
which are derived from facts and experience
as opposed to those which are derived from
pure reasoning. They saw how abstract systems, hypotheses, and experimental laws supplemented or contradicted each other. At the
same time they understood that reason and
science could never include all the universe.
The unfolding of rational and experimental
truths draws us on eternally upon a road that
is without end and that is ever further removed from the truths necessary for existence
itself. No matter how precise and numerous
the arguments of reason and the laws of our
sciences may be, they cannot give us the explanation of our destiny, our reasons for acting as we do, the ultimate secret of happiness.
We must avail ourselves of another method
of approach, that of "sentiment," of "the

heart," or, as we say to-day, of intuition. It is sentiment that reveals to us God, prayer, morality, goodness, humanity. And when reason and experience are not in agreement with the impulses of the heart, the fault lies with reason and experience.

Logical reason, experimental truth, spiritual intuition—these are the three forces that control our modern thought and that we attempt to-day to coördinate or to harmonize.

The history of thought in the eighteenth century is a complex history, and certain scholars have been quite wrong in attempting to simplify it. A good many average or mediocre persons blended confusedly without realizing the fact—often without desiring to realize the fact—diverging or even contradictory tendencies. Generally they were neither "entirely Voltaire" nor "entirely Rousseau." The *Philosophical Dreams* or the *Nightcap* of an L.-S. Mercier are in turn Voltairian tales and Rousseauistic effusions or meditations, an outpouring of sensibility. A Dubois-Fontanelle is persecuted because of an *Ericie, or the Vestal*, which is a play directed against the Church; and he composes in a genuinely Voltairian style certain *Phil-*

osophical Adventures in which he derides
Voltaire, Helvétius, d'Holbach, and Montesquieu. The complexity becomes still
greater if one studies not merely individuals
but the currents of public opinion. Of course,
there is a clearly outlined evolution in the
history of French thought in the eighteenth
century. Until about 1740 men are fond of
argumentation; from 1740 to 1760 the experimental sciences complete their triumph; after
1762 men's souls are moved and exalted by
sensibility. But the experimental spirit appears as early as the end of the seventeenth
century, while sensibility is evidenced as
early as 1740. Until the very end of the century rationalized reason, abstract truth, and
generalized systems still enjoy some degree of
prestige. The ardor of "sentimental souls"
never completely silences the irony of Voltairian criticism. If there are seventy-two editions
of the *Modern Héloïse* from 1762 to 1800,
there are more than fifty of *Candide* from
1758 to the Revolution. French thought in the
second half of the eighteenth century is
neither rational nor philosophical, neither
scientific nor experimental, neither sentimental nor mystical. It represents all these ten-

dencies, according to the environment or the individual, and at times in the same environment and in the same individual.

And French thought is so blended not merely in a few individuals but in a great many. Learning has more than won its social rights and the respect of almost every one, in spite of the disdain of the nobly born and of those in power; it has become more or less common property. There are perhaps not many more educated people in 1770 than in 1670. But educated people of the year 1670 generally retained the attitude of mere pupils; they thought all their lives as they were taught to think in their youth. Toward 1770 there are so many fashions of thought, so new, so variegated, so tempting, that no one form of thought can be imposed; a free choice must be permitted. Not only in literary or social spheres, not only in Paris but in all France, all the routes of modern thought have been definitely opened, and for all men.

INDEX OF AUTHORS AND OTHERS
CITED IN THE HISTORICAL NOTES

171